The Present Crisis
of the Holy See

By
Henry Cardinal Manning

Table of Contents

Progress of the Mystery of Iniquity	7
Antichrist	19
What Holds Back Antichrist	26
The Great Apostasy	39

Publishers Preface

This book was compiled from four lectures given by Henry Cardinal Manning in 1861 on the present crisis of the Catholic Church. He correctly saw that a grave crisis was approaching and described the theological basis of the Great Apostasy and the more common speculations of the Fathers and Doctors of the Church on this most important subject. Further in several places he cites the Universal Agreement of the Fathers of the Church, which we know to be an infallible guide in discerning the truth in doctrinal matters. This book is even more appropriate today, when many of these prophecies appear to be being fulfilled.

Saint Pius X Press

Author's Preface

TO THE VERY REVEREND
JOHN HENRY NEWMAN, P.D.
Of the Congregation of St. Philip Neri.
My Dear Dr. Newman.

About three years ago you kindly joined my name with your own in the dedication of your last volume of Sermons. Let me give a proof how grateful it was to um to be in any way united with you by asking you to let me join your name with mine in this unworthy return, but, as you know, the is the old bargain.

You were so kind as to own me as a friend of nearly thirty years; and that tells me that we are both touching upon the time of life when men may look back and measure the path they have trod. It is no small thing to have been in an active life of much eventfulness and labour for more than a quarter of a century, and for a full generation of man. With very few exceptions, all the men who held trust and power when our friendship began have passed away, and a new generation has been born and has up to manhood since we entered into life.

Men are always tempted to think the times in which they live eventful and pregnant beyond other; arts But, allowing for this common infirmity, I think we shall not he far wrong in considering exceptionally great the thirty years which, beginning with Catholic Emancipation, embrace the restoration of the Catholic Episcopate to England, and terminate with the antichristian movement of Europe against the Temporal Sovereignty of the Holy See. I may add, that to you and to me this period hi another high and singular interest in the intellectual movement which sprung up chiefly at Oxford, and has made itself felt throughout our country and our times. You have been a master-builder in this work, and I a witness of its growth. You remained long in Oxford, Mill with all its disfigurements so dear to both of us; but I was removed to a distance, and had to work alone. Nevertheless, to you I owe a debt of gratitude for intellectual help and light, greater than to any one man of our time; and it gives me a sincere gratification now publicly to acknowledge, though I can in no way repay, it. Among the many things which give a vivid and grave interest to this moment is the pronounced and explicit development on either side of the two great intellectual movement, the course of which we have watched so long. There was a time when those who now stand opposed as Catholics and Rationalists were apparently in close and perfect identity of conviction. But under the form of a common opinion there lay concealed, even then, the essential antagonism of two principles, the divergence of which is as wide as Divine faith or human opinion can interpose between the minds of men.

While every year has confirmed with luminous evidence the reason which, to you and to me, dented the convictions of intellect into the consciousness of faith, and has revealed to us the Divine unity and endowments of the only Church of God, some of those who were at our side, or sitting at your feet, have been carried back, as by a groundswell, into Anglicanism, Protestantism, Latitudinarianism, and rationalistic Deism. While the Divine character and sovereignty of the One Church Catholic and Roman, with the prerogatives of the Vicar of the In. Incarnate Word, have manifested themselves to us in an amplitude and majesty which commands the loving obedience a intellect, and heart, and will, and all the powers of our life, others we once loved well have come to find their chief claim to statesmanship in a policy which, to me, is simply the prelude of Antichrist. The Italian policy of England is without any other name. And I am amazed that the great French people, so sensitive of English preeminence, so jealous of English influence, and so justly contemptuous of the absurdities of English Protestantism, should have allowed itself to be goaded or gibed into accomplishing a policy hateful to Catholic France, and surpassing all the hopes of Protestant

England. To strip the Holy See of its temporal sovereignty has been since Henry VIII the passion of Protestant England; but it never dreamed of accomplishing its object of predilection by the hand of Catholic France. This is a surpassing achievement.

I had hardly written this sentence when I rend the debate in the House of Commons on the Foreign Policy of Government I do not think either you or I are likely to be suspected as apologists for the Neapolitan prisons, if they are us bad as ours were a few years ago; or for la torture de Naples, if there be in it a particle of truth, which I more than doubt. You and I have no fear of being thought to be lovers of despotism, or absolutism, or even of repressive government. But I think we shall both judge it to be a melancholy spectacle when we see the House of Commons led away by declamations on these topics from the laws which have created Christian Europe and all that is precious in the English constitution, to approve a policy subversive of European society. The law of nations public rights, established treaties, and legitimate possession, are no doubt to the modern school of statesmen null and without meaning. They are nevertheless the realities which hind society together; and they constitute the moral tests by which the justice of a cause is to be tried. The policy which violates them is immoral: its end is public lawlessness and its success will be its own punishment Now I have no deeper conviction than that this anticatholic movement, led or stimulated by England, will have its perfect success, and will reign for a time supreme; and next that, perhaps before we are in our graves all who have partaken in it—princes, statesmen and people—will be scourged by a universal conflict with revolution, and a European war, to which 1793 and the wars of the first empire are a faint prelude. What shames and alarms me most is to see that men, who once believed in a higher order of Christian politics, now propagate against the Holy See the doctrine of nationality, and the lawfulness of revolution, which, if applied to England. would only fail to dismember the empire because it would be put down in blood. It seems as if men had lost their light. How otherwise can we explain the blindness which cannot sce that the conflict of France and Austria has weakened the Catholic society of Europe, and has given to the Protestant politics of England and Prussia a most dangerous predominance? It will not be long before a European war will wear out and waste the powers of the Christian society including Protestant and Catholic alike, and will give a fatal predominance to the antichristian society, or revolution, which is every whore preparing for the last struggle, and for its supremacy. The Catholic society of Europe weakened, the

Christian society will soon in turn give way. Then comes the scourge. The conviction I feel that a great retribution is impending over the anticatholic movement of England, France, and Italy is rendered all the more certain by the fact hat the critical point in the whole conflict, the key of the whole and the last success to be gained is the dethronement of the Vicar of our Redeemer. The temporal power of the Pope, we are told, has been the great hindrance to the peace of Italy and Europe. It is this which distributes and marshals the two arrays. Qui non mecum, contra me est. They will have their day, and the Vicar of Jesus Christ will await his time. Si morain fecerit, expecta illum; quia vaniens veniet, et non tardabit.

Meanwhile England is preparing for its own dissolution. It has headed the unbelief of Europe, and it will be devoured by its own followers. The Reformation has done its work upon it. Protestantism, like the shirt of Nessus, cleaves to the flesh of England, and its day will come at last. We are told that man has some eighty-three parasites which live upon his substance. The Anglican Church in like manner gives pabulum to every heresy, and harbours within its system what the tiring Church of God expels and casts out. At this moment in the Established Church there exists in a formal state Pelagianims, Nestorianism, Calvinism, Lutheranism, Zuinglianism, Naturalism, and Rationalism. I pass over a multitude of other less formal heresies, and name only these because they have a definite and active existence in the Established, and are reproducing themselves. It is intrinsic enmity of this congeries of heresies which directs the political power of England against the Catholic Church, and, above all, against the Holy See; and gives to England the melancholy and bad preeminence of the most anticatholic and therefore the most antichristian, power of the world.

In the following pages I have endeavored, not for so great a subject most insufficiently, to show that what is passing in our times is the prelude of the antichristian period of the final dethronement of Christendom, and of the restoration of society without God in the world. But, sooner or later, so it must be. "The Son of Man indeed goeth, as it is written of Him; but woe to that man by whom the Son of Man shall be betrayed; it were better for him if that man had not been born" (St Matt. 26:24)

May God keep us from sharing even by silence in the persecution of His Church!

Believe me, my dear Dr. Newman, always affectionately yours.
E MANNING.
St. Mary's Baywater. Easter, 1861

Progress of the Mystery of Iniquity

I am well aware that the truths and principles of Revelation have been, by the common content of public men, formally excluded from the sphere of politics, and that to apply them as tests to the events of the world is regarded, in these days, as a weakness of mind. They who reject Revelation altogether are consistent in such a judgment; but with what consistency they who profess to believe in a revelation of the Divine government of the world, nevertheless consent to exclude it from the field of contemporaneous history, I cannot tell. I am, therefore, going, prudens et videns, to run counter to the popular spirit of these times, and it may be to expose myself to the contempt or compassion of those who believe the world to be governed by the action of the human will alone. To this I resign myself very willingly, and with no perturbation. My intention is, to examine the present relation of the Church to the civil powers of the world, by the light of a prophecy recorded by St. Paul, and to draw out certain principles of a practical kind, the direction of those who believe that the Divine will is also present in the events now taking place before our eyes.

I am not about to enter upon expositions of the Apocalypse, or to calculate the year of the end of the world. This I leave to those who may be called to it. The points I propose to take are few and practical; and the result I desire to attain is a clearer discernment of what principles are Christian, and what are Antichristian, and a surer appreciation of the character of the events by which the Church and the Holy See are at present tried.

St. Paul, writing to the Thessalonians, says: "Let no man deceive you by any means: for unless there come a revolt first, and the man of sin be revealed, the son of perdition, who opposeth, and is lifted up above all that is called God, or that is worshipped, so that he sitteth in the temple of God, showing himself as if he were God. Remember you not, that when I was yet with you, I told you these things? And now you know what withholdeth, that he may be revealed in his time. For the mystery of iniquity already worketh: only that he who now holdeth, do hold, until he be taken out of the way, and then that wicked one shall be revealed, whom the Lord Jesus shall kill with the spirit of His mouth, and shall destroy with the brightness of His coming: him, whose coining is according to the working of Satan, in all power, and signs, and lying wonders, and in all seduction of iniquity to them that perish: because they received not the love of the truth, that they might be saved. Therefore God shall send them the operation of error, to believe lying: that all may be judged who have not believed the truth, but have consented to iniquity:"[1]

We have here a prophecy of four great facts: first, of a revolt, which shall precede the second coming of our Lord; secondly, of the manifestation of one who is called "the wicked one;" thirdly, of hindrance which restrains his manifestation; and lastly, of the period of power and persecution, of which he will be the author.

In treating of this subject, I shall not venture upon any conjectures of my own, but shall deliver simply what I find either in the Fathers of the Church, or in such theologians as the Church has recognised, namely, Bellarmine, Lessius, Malvenda, Viegas, Suarez, Ribera, and others.

First, then, what is the revolt? In the original it is called an apostasy; and in the Vulgate, discessio, or a departure. Now a revolt implies a seditious separation from some authority, and a consequent opposition to it.[2]

If we can find the authority, we shall find perhaps also the revolt.

Now there are in the world but two ultimate authorities, the civil and the spiritual, and this revolt must be either a sedition or schism. Moreover, it must be something upon a wide field, and in proportion to the terms and events of the prediction.

St. Jerome, with some others, interprets this revolt to be the rebellion of the nations or provinces against the Roman Empire. He says, Nisi venerit discessio. . . . ut omnes gentes quae Romano Imperio subjacent, recedant ab eis; an interpretation we need not examine, forasmuch as the events of Christian history refute it. They have revolted, and no manifestation has appeared. It seems to need link proof that this revolt or apostasy or separation, not from the civil, but from the spiritual order and authority; for the sacred writers, again and again, speak of such a spiritual separation; and in one place St. Paul seems expressly to declare the meaning of this word. He forewarns St. Timothy that in the later days, "some shall depart or apostatize from the faith;" and it seems evident that the same spiritual falling away is intended by the apostasy in this place.

The authority, then, from which the revolt is to take place is that of the kingdom of God on earth, prophesied by Daniel as the kingdom which

---

[1] II Thessalonians 2:3-11
[2] See 'History of the Church; Formation of the Apostles of the Latter days' by Friedl. St. Pius X Press www.stpiusxpress.com

the God of heaven should set up after the four kingdoms should be destroyed by the stone cut out without hands, which became a great mountain and filled the whole earth; or, in other words, the one and universal Church, founded by our Divine Lord, and spread by His Apostles throughout the world. In this one only supernatural kingdom was deposited the true and pure theism, or knowledge of God, and the true and only faith of God incarnate, with the doctrines and laws of grace. This, then, is the authority from which the revolt is to be made, be that revolt what it may.

Such being the authority against which the revolt is made, it cannot be difficult to ascertain its character. The inspired writers expressly describe its notes.

The first is, schism, as given by St John: "It is the last hour: and as you have heard that Antichrist cometh: even now there are become many Antichrists: whereby we know that it is the last hour. They went out from us; but they were not of us for if they had been of us, they would no doubt have remained with us." [3]

The second note is, the rejection of the office and presence of the Holy Ghost. St. Jude says "These are they, who separate themselves, sensual men" (animal or merely rational and natural men) "having not the spirit:" [4] This necessarily involves the heretical principle of human opinion as opposed to Divine faith; of the private spirit as opposed to the infallible voice of the Holy Ghost, speaking through the Church of God.

The third note is the denial of the Incarnation. St John writes "Every spirit, which confesseth that Jesus Christ is come in the flesh is of God: and every spirit that dissolveth Jesus" (that is, by denying the mystery of the Incarnation, either the true Godhead, or the true manhood, or the unity or divinity of the person of the Incarnate Son) "is not of God, and this is Antichrist, of whom you have heard that he cometh, and he is now already in the world." [5] Again he says, "Many seducers are gone out into the world, who confess not that Jesus Christ is come in the flesh: this is a seducer and an Antichrist." [6]

These, then, are the marks by which, as the Church is to be known by her notes, the antichristian revolt, or apostasy, may be distinguished.

---

[3] I John 2:18-19
[4] Jude 19
[5] John 4:2-3
[6] 2 John 7

We will now see whether they can be verified in the history of Christianity, or in the present position of the Church in the world.

The first point to notice is, that both St. Paul and St. Peter speak of this antichristian revolt as already begun in their own day.

St. Paul says, "The mystery of iniquity already worketh: only that he who now holdeth do hold, until he be taken out of the way." [7] And St John expressly in the above-quoted places: "It is the last hour: and as you have heard that Antichrist cometh, even now there are become many Antichrists: whereby we know that it is the last hour." [8] Again. "This is Antichrist, of whom you have heard that he cometh; and he is now already in the world." [9]

We must look, then, for the beginnings of this revolt in the times of the Apostles The spirit of Antichrist was at work as soon as Christ was manifested to the world. in one word, then, it describes the continuous working of the spirit of heresy, which from the beginning has run parallel to the faith.

It is evident that St. Paul and St. John applied these terms to the Nicolaitans, the Gnostics, and the like. The three notes of Antichrist, schism, heresy, and the denial of the Incarnation, were manifest in them. It is equally applicable to the Sabellian, Arian, Semiarian, Monophysite, Monethelite, Eutychian, and Macedonian heresies The principles are identical; the development various but only accidental. And so, throughout these eighteen hundred years, every successive heresy has generated schism, and every schism has generated heresy; and all alike deny the Divine Voice of the Holy Ghost speaking continuously through the Church; and all alike substitute human opinion for Divine faith; and all alike work out, by a sure process, some more rapidly, and some more slowly, a denial of the Incarnation of the Eternal Son. Some may start with it in the outset others resolve themselves into it by a long and unforeseen transmutation, as that of Protestantism into Rationalism; but all being identical in principle, are identical also in their consequences. Every age has its heresy, as every article of faith by denial receives its definition; and the course of heresy is measured and periodical; varies materially, but formally one, both in principle and action; so that all the heresies from the beginning are no more than the continuous development and expansion of "the mystery of iniquity," which was already at work.

---

[7] II Thessalonians 2:7
[8] I John 2:18
[9] I John 4:7

Another phenomenon in the history of heresy is its power of organising and perpetuating itself, at least until it resolves itself into some more subtle and aggressive form: for instance, Arianism, which rivaled the Catholic Church in Constantinople. Lombardy, and Spain; Donatism, which equaled the Church in Africa; Nestorianism, which outnumbered the Church in Asia; Mahometanism, which punished and absorbed most of its forerunners, and established, in the East and South, the most terrible antichristian military power the world has ever seen; and Protestantism, which has organized itself into a vast political antagonist to the Holy See, not only in the North, but by its policy and diplomacy even in Catholic countries.

To this power of expansion must be added a certain morbid and noxious reproduction. Physiologists tell us that there is a perfect ultimate unity even in the countless diseases which devour the body; nevertheless, each disease seems to throw out its progeny by a corruption and reproduction. So in the history and development of heresy. To name no more than these,—Gnosticism, Arianism, and, above all, Protestantism, have generated each a multitude of subordinate and affiliated heresies. But it is Protestantism which, above all others, bears the three notes of the inspired writers in the greatest breadth and evidence. Other heresies have opposed parts and details of the Christian faith and Church; but Protestantism, taken in its historical complex, as we now are able, with the retrospect of three hundred years, to measure it, reaching from the religion of Luther, Calvin, and Cranmer at the one end, so the Rationalism and Pantheism of England and Germany at the other, is of all the most formal, detailed, and commensurate antagonist of Christianity. I do not mean that it has as yet attained its full development, for we shall see reasons to believe that it is still pregnant with a darker future; but even as "the mystery of iniquity" has already worked, no other antagonist has as yet gone so deep in undermining the faith of the Christian world.

I am not now pretending to write a treatise on the reproductiveness of Protestantism. It is enough to set down certain facts self-evident in the intellectual history of the last three hundred years, namely, that Socinianism, Rationalism, and Pantheism are the legitimate offspring of the Lutheran and Calvinistic heresies; and that Protestant England, the least intellectual and consistent of Protestant countries, affords as this moment a ready pabulum for the communication and reproduction of these spirits of error.

All that I wish to point out is, to use a modern phrase, that the movement of heresy is one and the same from the beginning: that the Gnostics were the Protestants of their day, and the Protestants the Gnostics of ours; that the principle is identical, and the bulk of the movement unfolded to greater proportions; and its successes accumulated, and its antagonism to the Catholic Church changeless and essential. There are two consequences of operations of this movement so strange and so full of importance, as bearing upon its relation to the Church, that I cannot pass them by.

The first is, the development and worship of the principle of nationality, which has always been found in combination with heresy.

Now, the Incarnation abolished all national distinctions within the sphere of grace, and the Church absorbed all nations into its supernatural unity. One Fountain of spiritual jurisdiction, and one Divine Voice held together the wills and actions of a family of nations. Sooner or later, every heresy has identified itself with the nation in which it arose It has lived by the support of civil powers, and they have embodied the claim of national independence.

This movement, which is the key of the so-called great Western schism, is the rationale also of the Reformation; and the but three hundred years have given a development and intensity to the spirit of separate nationalism, of which we as yet see no more than the preludes. I need not point out how this nationalism is essentially schismatical, which is to be seen not only in the Anglican Reformation, but in the Gallican liberties and the contentions of Portugal in Europe and in India, to name no more.

Now I have pointed out this result of heresy because it verifies one of the three marks above mentioned. If heresy in the individual dissolves the unity of the Incarnation, heresy in a nation dissolves the unity of the Church, which is built upon the Incarnation. And in this we see a truer and deeper meaning of the words of St. Jerome than he foresaw himself. It is not the revolt of nations from the Roman Empire, but the apostasy of nations from the kingdom of God, which was set up on its ruins. And this process of national defection, which began openly with the Protestant Reformation, is running its course, as we shall see hereafter, even in nations still nominally Catholic; and the Church is putting off its medieval character as the mother of nations, returning again into its primitive condition as a society of members scattered among the peoples and cities of the world.

The other result I spoke of as the consequence of the later workings of the heretical spirit is the deification of humanity. This we have before us in two distinct forms, namely, in the Pantheistic and in the Positive philosophies; or rather in the religion of Positivism, the last aberration of Comte.

It would be impossible in this place to give an adequate account of these two final developments of unbelief; to do so would need a treatise. It will be enough to express, in a popular way, the outline of these two forms of antichristian impiety.

I take the expression of the Pantheism of Germany from two of its modem expositors, in whom it may be said to culminate. We are told that, "Before the time when creation began, we may imagine that an infinite mind, an infinite essence, or an infinite thought (for here all these are one), filled the universe of space. This, then, as the self existent One, must be the only absolute reality; all else can be but a developing of the one original and eternal being. ... This primary essence is not ... an infinite substance, having the two properties of extension and thought, but an infinite, acting, producing, self-unfolding mind—the living soul of the world."

"If we can view all things as the development of the original and absolute principle of life, reason, or being, then it is evident conversely that we may trace the marks of the absolute in every thing that exists, and consequently may scan them in the operation of our own minds, as one particular phase of its manifestation."

"In practical philosophy we have three movements: the first is that in which the active intelligence shows itself operating within limited circuit, as in a single mind. This is the principle of individuality, not as though the infinite intelligence were something different from the finite, or as though there were an infinite intelligence out of and apart from the finite, but it is merely the absolute in one of its particular moments; just as an individual thought is but a single moment of the whole mind. Each finite reason, then, is but a thought of the infinite and eternal reason." The absolute essence being thus every thing, all difference between God and the universe is truly lost; and Pantheism becomes complete, "as the absolute is evolved from its lowest form to the highest, in accordance with the necessary law or rhythm of its being, the whole world, material and mental, becoming one enormous chain of necessity, to which no idea of free creation can be attached. Again: "Deity is a process ever going on but never accomplished, nay, the Divine consciousness is absolutely one with the advancing consciousness of mankind. The hope of immortality perishes; for death is but the return of the individual to the infinite, and man is annihilated, though the Deity will eternally live." Once more: "Deity is the eternal process of self-development as realised in man; the Divine and human consciousness falling absolutely together." "The knowledge of God and of his manifestations forms the subject of speculative theology... . Of these manifestations there art three great spheres of observation—nature, mind, and humanity. In nature we see the Divine idea in its lowest expression; in mind, with its powers, faculties, moral feelings, freedom, etc., we see it in its higher and more perfect form; lastly, in humanity we see God not only as creator and sustainer, but also as a father and a guide." "The soul is a perfect mirror of the universe, and we have only to gaze into it with earnest attention to discover all truth which is accessible to humanity. What we know of God, therefore, can be only that which is originally revealed to us of Him in our own minds"; I have given these extracts to show the legitimate resolution of the subjective system of private judgment into pure rationalistic Pantheism.

With a few words on the Positivism of Comte, I will conclude. Lest I should appear to distort or colour this form of aberration, I will give it in the author's own words

First, then, he describes the Positive philosophy as follows:

"From the study of the development of human intelligence, in all directions and through all times, the discovery arises of a great fundamental law, to which it is necessarily subject, and which has a solid foundation of proof, both in the facts of our organisation and in our historical experience. The law is this: that each of our leading conceptions, each branch of our knowledge, passes successively through three different theoretical conditions—the Theological or fictitious; the Metaphysical or abstract; and the Scientific or positive. In other words, the human mind by its nature employs in its progress three methods of philosophising, the character of which is essentially different and even radically opposed, viz the theological method, the metaphysical, and the positive. Hence arise three philosophies, or general systems of conceptions, on the aggregate of phenomena, each of which excludes the others. The first is the necessary point of departure of the human understanding, and the third is its fixed and definite state. The second is merely a state of transition.

"In the theological state, the human mind, seeking the essential nature of beings, the first and final causes (the origin and purpose) of all effects,—in short, absolute knowledge,—supposes all phenomena to be produced by the immediate action of supernatural beings.

"In the metaphysical state, which is only a modification of the first, the mind supposes, instead of supernatural beings, abstract forces, veritable entities (that is, personified abstractions), inherent in all beings, and capable of producing all phenomena. What is called the explanation of phenomena is, in this stage, a mere reference of each to its proper entity.

"In the final, the positive state, the mind has given over the search after absolute notions, the origin and destination of the universe, and the causes of phenomena, and applies itself to the study of their laws, that is, their invariable relations of succession and resemblance. Reasoning and observation, duly combined, are the means of this knowledge. What is now understood when we speak of an explanation of facts, is simply the establishment of a connection between single phenomena and some general facts, the number of which continually diminishes with the progress of science." [10]

From this it will be observed that the belief in God has passed into the first or fictitious period of the human reason.

Nevertheless, after the completion of his Philosophy, Comte perceived the necessity of a religion.

Hence the Catechism of Positive Religion, which thus begins: "In the name of the Past and of the Future, the servants of Humanity—both its philosophical and practical servants—come forward to claim as their due the general direction of this world. Their object is to constitute at length a real Providence in all departments, moral, intellectual, and material. Consequently they exclude, once for all, from political supremacy all the different servants of God—Catholic. Protestant, or Deist— as being at once behindhand and a cause of disturbance: [11]

But inasmuch as there can be no religion without worship, and no worship without a God, and inasmuch as there is no God, Comte had need to find or to create a Divinity. Now as there is no God, there can be no being higher than man, and no object of worship higher than mankind. "The imaginary beings whom religion provisionally introduced for its purposes were able to inspire lively affections in man—affections which were even most powerful under the least elaborate of the fictitious systems. The immense scientific preparation required as an introduction to Positivism for a long time seemed to deprive it of any such valuable

---

[10] Positive Philosophy, vol. e. I.
[11] Catechism or Positive Religion, Preface

aptitude. Whilst the philosophical initiation only comprehended the order of the material world, nay, even when it had extended to the order of living beings, it could only reveal laws which were indispensable for our action; it could not furnish us with any direct object for an enduring and constant affection. This is no longer the case since the completion of our gradual preparation by the introduction of the special study of the order of mans existence, whether as an individual or as a society. This is the last step in the process. We are now able to condense the whole of our Positive conceptions in the one single idea of an immense and eternal Being. Humanity, destined by sociological laws to constant development under the preponderating influence of biological and cosmological necessities. This the real great Being, on whom all, whether individuals or societies, depend as the prime mover of their existence, becomes the centre of our affections. They rest on it by as spontaneous an impulse as do our thoughts and our actions This Being, by its very idea, suggests at once the sacred formula of Positivism;—Love as our principle, Order as our basis, and Progress as our end. Its compound existence is ever founded on the free concurrence of independent wills. All discord tends to dissolve that existence, which, by its very notion, sanctions the constant predominance of the heart over the intellect, as the sole basis of our true unity. So the whole order of things henceforth finds its expression in the being who studies it, and who is ever perfecting it. The struggle of Humanity against the combined influences of the necessities it is obliged to obey, growing as it does in energy and success, offers the heart, no less than the intellect, a better object of contemplation than the capricious omnipotence of its theological precursor—capricious by the very force of the word omnipotence. Such a Supreme Being is more within the reach of our feelings as well as of our conceptions, for it is identical in nature with its servants at the same time that it is superior to them." [12]

You must define Humanity as the whole of human beings, past, present, and future The word whole points out clearly that you must not take in all men, but those only who are really capable of assimilation, in virtue of a real cooperation on their part in furthering the common good. All are necessarily born children of Humanity, but all do not become her servants. Many remain in the parasitic state, which, excusable during their education, becomes blamable when that education is complete. Times of anarchy bring forth in swarms such creatures, nay, even enable them to

---

[12] Catechism of Positive Religion, pp. 63, 74.

flourish, though they are, in sad truth, but burdens on the true Great Being." It will be observed that both Pantheism and Positivism alike end in the deification of man: they are a boundless egotism and an apotheosis[13] of human pride.

I shall not dwell further on this point; and mention it only because I shall have to refer to it hereafter.

I will now briefly sum up what I have said.

We see that it is foretold, that, before the manifestation of the last great antagonist of God and of His incarnate Son, there must be a revolt and falling away; we have seen that the authority from which the revolt is to be made is manifestly that of the Church of God, and that it will be a revolt bearing the three notes of schism, heresy, and denial of the Incarnation; we see also that this Antichristian movement was at work even in the days of the Apostles; that it has wrought ever since in manifold forms and various times, and with most diverse, and even contradictory, developments, but that nevertheless it is always one and the same, identical in principle and in antagonism to the Incarnation and to the Church. It is evident that this movement has accumulated its results from age to age, and that at this time it is more mature and has a loftier stature and a greater power and a more formal antagonism to the Church and the faith than ever before.

It has attached itself to the pride of governments by nationalism, and of individuals by philosophy, and, under the forms of Protestantism, Civilisation, Secularism, it has organised a vast Anticatholic power in the east, north, and west of Europe. As a matter of fact, Catholic and Anticatholic describe the two arrays. I am afraid I must add, Christian and Antichristian. And this is one of my purposes in treating of the subject before us; for I am convinced that multitudes are carried away, not knowing whither they go, by a movement essentially opposed to all their best and deepest convictions, because they are unable to discern its real ultimate principle and character.

In the present array of the popular opinion of Europe against the Holy See and the Vicar of Jesus Christ, may be discerned the Antichristian instinct. The revolutions in Italy, backed by the anticatholic spirit of the continent, and by the policy of England, are fulfilling the prophecies, and confirming our faith. But this I shall hope to show more fully hereafter. It seems inevitable that the enmity of all nations which are separated from

---

[13] From the Greek 'to deify'

the Catholic unity, and penetrated by the spirit of the Reformation, that by the spirit of private judgment as opposed to the Divine Voice of the living Church, and by the unbelief which has banished the Eucharistical presence of the Incarnate Word, should be concentrated upon the person who is the Vicar and Representative of Jesus, and upon the Body which witnesses alone for the Incarnation, and for all its mysteries of truth and grace. Such is the one Holy Catholic and Roman Church, and such is the Supreme Pontiff, its Visible Head. Such, in the words of Holy Scripture, are the two mysteries of godliness and of iniquity. All things are throwing out into light and prominence the two ultimate powers, which divide the destinies of men. The conflict is a simple antagonism of Christ and Antichrist; and the two arrays are marshalling in order, and men are choosing their principles; or events are choosing for them; and they are drifting unconsciously into currents, of which they are not aware. The theory, that politics and religion have different spheres is an illusion and a snare. For history can only be truly read in the light of faith; and the present can only be interpreted by the light of revelation; for above the human wills which are now in conflict, there is a Will, sovereign and divine, which is leading all things to fulfil its own perfect end.

Antichrist

Such, then, is the Revolt, which has been gathering strength these 1800 years, and ripening for the hour when it shall receive its leader and head.

The interpretation universally received by anti-catholic controversialists, whereby, first Antichrist is held to be a spirit or system, and not a person, and next, to be the Catholic or Roman Church, or the Vicar of the Incarnate Word, is the masterstroke of deceit. It allays all fear, and inspires presumption and confidence, and fixes the attention of men to watch for the signs of his appearing any where except where they are to be seen; and draws it off from the quarter where they are already visible.

Now, I do not hesitate to say, that, in all the prophecies of Revelation, there is not one among them, which relates to the coming of Christ more explicit and express than those, which relate to the coming of Antichrist.

1. He is described with all the attributes of a person. In this one passage St. Paul calls him that wicked one; the man of sin; and son of perdition. And St. John in four places speaks of him as the Antichrist. To deny the personality of Antichrist, is therefore to deny the plain testimony of Holy Scripture: to explain away these personal terms and titles as of a system or spirit, is as rationalistic as the impiety of Strauss in denying "the historical," that is, the personal Christ.

It is a law of Holy Scripture, that when persons are prophesied of, persons appear, as, for instance, the prophecies of St. John Baptist, or of the Blessed Virgin, or of our Lord Himself.

All the Fathers, both of the East and West,—St. Tremens, St. Cyprian, St. Jerome, St. Ambrose. St. Cyril of Jerusalem, St. Gregory of Nazianzum, St. John Chrysostom. Theophylact, Ecumenius,—all interpret these passages of a literal and personal Antichrist. What I may call the corporate interpretation is modern, heretical, controversial, and unreasonable. This fanciful and contradictory system has been sufficiently destroyed even by Protestant writers: as by Todd in his work on Antichrist, a creditable and learned book, though somewhat defaced by the reliquiae of Protestant prejudice; by Creswell, in his Exposition of the Parables; and by Maitland on Daniel and St. John. In Germany even among Protestant interpreters, to maintain the anticatholic interpretation is looked on as a surrender of the character of a biblical scholar. The

Protestants of England are still, as they always were, the least cultivated and reasonable. It is true, indeed, that the Antichrist has had, and may still have, many forerunners, as had also Christ Himself: as Isaac, Moses, Josue, David, Jeremias, were types of the one, so Antiochus, Julian, Arius, Mahomet, and many more, are the types of the other; for persons typify persons. So, again. as Christ is the Head and Representative in which the whole mystery of godliness has been summed up and recapitulated, so also the whole mystery of impiety will find its expression and its head in the person of Antichrist. He may indeed embody a spirit and represent a system, but is not less, therefore, a person. So also the theologians. Bellarmine says, "All Catholics hold that Antichrist will be one individual person." [14] Lessius says, "All agree in teaching that the proper Antichrist will be not many, but one only person."[15] Suarez goes so far as to say that this doctrine of the personal Antichrist of faith is "certain de fide."

    2. Next, the Fathers believed that Antichrist will be of the Jewish race. Such was the opinion of St. Irenaeus, St. Jerome, and of the author of the work De Consummatione Mundi, ascribed to St. Hippolytus, and of a writer of a Commentary on the Epistle to the Thessalonians, ascribed to St. Ambrose, of many others, who add, that he will be of the tribe of Dan: as, for instance, St. Gregory the Great, Theodoret, Aretas of Caesarea, and many more. Such also is the opinion of Bellarmine, who calls it certain. Lessius affirms that the Fathers, with unanimous consent, teach as undoubted, that Antichrist will be a Jew. Ribera repeats the same opinion, and adds that Aretas, St. Bede, Haymo, St. Anselm, and Rupert affirm that for this reason the tribe of Dan is not numbered among those who are sealed in the Apocalypse. Viegas says the same quoting other authorities. And this will appear probable, if we consider that the Antichrist will come to deceive the Jews, accenting to the prophecy of our Lord "I am come in My Father's name, and you receive Me not: another will come in his own name, him you will receive;" which words are interpreted by the Fathers with one consent of the false Messias, who shall pass himself off upon the Jews as the true. And this, again, is the unanimous interpretation of the Fathers, both of the East and of the West, us St. Cyril of Jerusalem, St. Ephrem Syrus, St. Gregory Nazianzen, St. Gregory Nyssen, St. John Damascene, and also of St. Irenaeus, St. Cyprian, St. Jerome, St. Ambrose, and St. Augustine. The probability of this also will appear, if we consider, further, that a false Christ would fail of the first condition of success if he

---
[14] De Summo Pontifice Book 3, c 2
[15] de Anticristo

were not of the house of David; that the Jews are still looking out for coming; that they have prepared themselves for delusion by crucifying the true Messias; and therefore it is that the Fathers interpret of the true Messias and the false the words of St Paul to the Thessalonians: "Because they received not the love of the truth, that they might be saved; therefore God shall send them the operation of error to believe lying." [16]

Now, I think no one can consider the dispersion and providential preservation of the Jews among all nations of the world, the indestructible vitality of their race, without believing that they are reserved for some future action of His judgment and grace. And this is foretold again and again in the New Testament; for instance, in the Epistles to the Romans and the Corinthians. [17]

3. From this we perceive a third character of Antichrist, namely, that he will not be simply the antagonist, but the substitute or supplanter of the true Messias: And this is rendered still more probable by the fact, that the Messias looked for by the Jews has always been a temporal deliverer, the restorer of their temporal order; or, in other words, a political and military prince. It is obvious also, that whosoever may hereafter deceive them in the pretended character of their Messias, must thereby deny the Incarnation, whatsoever claim to a supernatural character he may put forward for himself. In his own person he will be a complete denial of the whole Christian faith and Church; for if he be the true Messias, the Christ of the Christians must be false.

Now, perhaps, we do not sufficiently realize how commonplace and historical a person such a deceiver may be. We are so possessed with the idea and vision of the true Messias in the glory of His Godhead and Manhood, of His Divine actions and Passion, of His Resurrection, Ascension, and royalties over the world and the Church, that we cannot conceive how any false Christ could be received as the true. It is for this reason that our Lord has made of these latter times: "There shall arise false Christs and false prophets, insomuch as to deceive (if possible) even the elect;" [18] that is, they shall not be deceived; but those who have lost faith in the Incarnation, such as humanitarian's rationalists, and pantheists, may well be deceived by any person of great political power and success who should restore the Jews to their own land, and people Jerusalem once more with the sons of the patriarchs. And there is nothing in the political aspect

---

[16] II Thessalonians 2:10-11
[17] Romans 11:-15-24; II Corinthians 3:16
[18] Matthew 24:24

of the world which renders such a combination impossible; indeed, the state of Syria, and the title of European diplomacy, which is continually moving eastward, render such an event within reasonable probability.

4. But the prophecies assign to the person of Antichrist a more preternatural character. He is described as a worker of false miracles. His coming is said to be "according to the working of Satan, in all power, and signs, and lying wonders and all seduction of iniquity to them that perish."[19]

And here I cannot but perceive a wonderful change, which has passed upon the world. Half a century ago the men who rejected Christianity derided a belief in witchcraft as superstition. and in miracles as foolishness. But now the world has outstripped even the faith of Christians by its credulity. Europe and America are deluged by Spiritualism. I know not how many hundreds and thousands of mediums between us and the unseen world are in existence. The very men who would not permit the witch of Endor, or Elymas the sorcerer, to pass without ridicule, believe in table turning and table-rapping, in clairvoyance, and the communications of spirits evoked from the world unseen; in spirit-writing, and locomotion through the air, and in the apparition of hands, and even of personal Revelation of the state of the dead, of secrets among the living, prolonged and repeated colloquies with the departed, are not only believed, but practiced habitually, and almost day by day. Now it is not my object, at least not now, to appreciate these phenomena. It is enough for us to say, that to us who believe in an unseen world and in the presence and warfare of spirits, good and evil, such things present no difficulty. We are not disposed to deny their reality because of the falsehood or delusion, which is mixed up with them. They are precisely what the Church has always condemned and forbidden under the name of witchcraft: in which there is a real preternatural agency surrounded by much imposture. I dwell on this point because it is certain that we are encompassed by a supernatural order, of which part is divine, and part is diabolical. It is not wonderful that they who reject the divine supernatural order should become immoderately credulous of the diabolical. Now in this we have already a preparation for the deception of which St. Paul writes. The age is ripe for a delusion. It will not believe the miracles of the saints, but it will copiously drink down the phenomena of spiritualism. A successful medium might well pass himself off by his

---

[19] II Thessalonians 2:9-10

preternatural endowments as the promised Messias, and "signs and lying wonders" in abundance may be wrought by the agencies which are already abroad in the world.

5. The last characteristic of which I will speak is more difficult, perhaps, to conceive. St. Paul says of "the man of sin," "the son of perdition, who opposeth, and is lifted up above all that is called God, or that is worshiped; so that he sitteth in the temple of God, showing himself as if he were God." These words are interpreted by the Fathers to mean that he will claim divine honers, and that in the Temple of Jerusalem. St. Irenaeus says that "Antichrist being an apostate and a robber, will claim to be adored as God," and "that he will endeavour to show himself off as God! Lactantius, that "he will call himself God." The writer under the name of St. Ambrose says, "He will affirm himself to be God." St. Jerome, "He will call himself God, and claim to be worshiped by all." St. John Chrysostom "He will profess himself to be the God of all, and call himself and show himself off as God." So also Theodoret, Theophylact, Ecumenius, St. Anselm, and many others.

Suarez, in explaining this passage, says, "It is likely that Antichrist will in no way believe himself what he will teach and compel others to believe. For though in the beginning he may persuade the Jews that he is the Messias and is sent from God, and may pretend to believe that the law of Moses is true and to be observed, yet he will do all this in dissimulation, to deceive them and to obtain supreme power. For afterwards he will reject the law of Moses, and will deny the true God who gave it. For which reason many believe that he will craftily destroy idolatry in order to deceive the Jews." "How great his perfidy will be, and what he will really believe concerning God, we cannot conjecture. But it is likely that he will be an atheist, and will deny both reward and punishment in another life, and will venerate only the preternatural being, from whom he has learned the art of deceit and acquired his riches, by which wealth he will obtain supreme power."

Now, it is easy to understand how he will oppose God, being the antagonist of Christ; and how he will exalt or lift himself above all that is called God and worshiped; because, in supplanting the true Messias, he places himself in the stead of the Incarnate God. Nor is it difficult to understand how those who have lost the true and divine idea of the Messias may accept a false one; and, being dazzled by the greatness of political and military successes, and inflated with the pantheistic and Socinian notions of the dignity of man. may pay to the person of

Antichrist the honor which Christians pay to the true Messias. I have touched on this because St. Paul places it prominently in the description of Antichrist, and because the tendency of the credulous unbelief, which increases in the world as faith decreases, is visibly preparing men for delusion.

It is one of the most wonderful interpretations of the Fathers, that in the end of the world paganism shall be restored. This at least we should have thought impossible: if for no other reason, at least from the development of modern infidelity; and yet infidelity was never more dominant than when in the first French Revolution revelation was voted to be false, and the worship of Reason and Ceres set up in its place. In truth, when the intellectual become pantheists, the simple will become polytheists. They need a more material conception than the refined unbelievers, and they impersonate and embody, first in thought and then in form, the object of their worship. And what is this but paganism simple and pure? But into this I cannot enter. In the second livraison [20] of Gaume's work on the French Revolution, especially in the 12th, 13th, and 14th chapters, will be found an ample and detailed account of the paganism of fifty years ago; and in the Catechism of Positive Religion, under the head of "Public and Private Worship"; will be seen an elaborate profession of religious worship addressed to humanity—the collective body of deified men, which is the natural basis of the religion of ancient Greece and Rome.

Now, I do not say that there may not be far more stupendous and preternatural phenomena about the manifestation and person of Antichrist. All history would lead us to expect it; all the prophecies seem to predict it; the great periods of divine action in the world foreshadow it. My object has not been to divest the future of the supernatural, but to show how the supernatural mingles itself in the ordinary course of the world, and steals upon us, so to speak, unawares "The kingdom of God cometh not with observation," but is in the midst of us, in full presence and power, under aspects which seem to us common and unmarked, in the currents of human action. in national movements, in the policy of governments, and the diplomacy of the world. As Christ at His coming was believed to be the carpenter, so Antichrist may be visibly no more than a successful adventurer. Even his preternatural character, true or false, may pass either as scintillations of insanity, or as the absurdities of his partisans, or the

---

[20] one of the numbers of a book published in parts

delusions of his flatterer. So the world blinds its own eyes by the fumes of its own intellectual pride. There is nothing out of the context or proportion, that a person should arise of Jewish blood, naturalized in some of the peoples of Europe, protector of the Jews, the purse-bearers, and journalists, and telegraphic wires, of the revolutions of Europe, hailed by them as their saviour from the social and political dominion of the Christians, surrounded by the phenomena of antichristian and anticatholic spiritualism, an arch-medium himself, and professing to be more than either Moses or Mahomet, that is, more than of human stature and proportion.

To those who have never discerned the ultimate unity in principle and action of truth, on the one side, and of falsehood, on the other, and likewise respectively of good and evil, it may appear strange to attach much importance to any event the sphere of which seems to be the Jewish race. But to those who believe that the world may be divided into Christian and Antichristian or Catholic and Anticatholic, or, in other words, into the natural order, based upon the mere human will and action, and the supernatural, based on the Divine will and the Incarnation of God, —it will at once be seen to be the question most vital and decisive of all. I shall hope to show hereafter that the antagonism between two persons is an antagonism also between two societies, and that as our Divine Lord is the Head and Representative of all the truth and justice of the world from the beginning, so Antichrist, be he who or what he may, will be the head and representative of all the falsehood and wrong, which has been accumulating for these 1800 years, in the heresies, schisms, spiritual editions, intellectual infidelities, social disorders and political revolutions of the anti-catholic movement of the world.

Such is the great deep upon which the Christian society of the world is resting. From time to time it has lifted itself up with preternatural power, and has made the Christian order of Europe vibrate and reel. Then again it has seemed to subside into a calm. But no one with any discernment can fail to see that it is deeper, mightier, and more widely spread now than ever. That this antichristian power will one day find its head, and for a time prevail in this world, is certain from prophecy. But this cannot be until "he who holdeth" shall be taken out of the way. This, however, is the next subject in our order, and I must not anticipate it here.

What Holds Back Antichrist?

Before I enter on our third subject, let us call to mind the two points which. I hope, have been established in what I have hitherto said. The first is, that we see the revolt, or falling away, already verified and manifested in the spiritual separation from the Church, and in the opposition to its Divine authority and its Divine voice, which we traced in operation from the day when the Apostle said, "The mystery of iniquity doth already work;' and St. John declared the Antichrists were already gone out into the world. The other point we have seen is this, that the man of sin, the non of perdition—the wicked one—is a person, in all probability, of the Jewish race; that he is to be supplanter of the true Messiah, and therefore an Antichrist in the sense of substituting himself in the place of the true, —a worker of false miracles, and claiming for himself Divine worship.

Now the third point on which I have to speak is the hindrance which retards his manifestation The Apostle says, "The mystery of iniquity doth already work; only that he who now holdeth" (that is, stands in the way of the revelation of the man of sin) "hold until" (the time that) "he be taken out of the way." As there is perpetual working of this mystery of iniquity, so there is a perpetual hindrance or barrier to its full manifestation, which will continue until it be removed; and there a fixed time when it shall be taken out of the way. St. Paul, in this passage, uses two expressions. He says the hindrance "which holdeth," and "who holdeth." He speaks of it as of a thing and as of a person. At first sight there appears to be a difficulty, whether that which hinders the revelation of the man of sin be a person or a system; for in the one place it is spoken of in the neuter as a system, in the other case it is spoken of in the masculine as a person. I hope in what I have hitherto said that I have already given a solution to this apparent difficulty. You will remember that I drew out shortly the parallel of the two mysteries of godliness and of iniquity, and of their respective heads. This is, in fact, the argument of St. Augustine, who has sketched the two mysteries of godliness and of iniquity, from the beginning of the world, under the character of the two cities—that is, the Spirit of God and the spirit of Satan, working by a manifold operation either in the elect servants of God, or in the enemies of God and of His Kingdom. And just as the mystery of godliness is summed up in the person and Incarnation of the Son of God, so the mystery of iniquity is summed up in the man of sin, who shall be revealed in his time. In like manner also, that which hinders, or he who hinders will be be found to express both a system and a person, and the person and the system to be identified after the same manner as the examples which I have already given.

First of all let us consider more particularly what is the character of "this wicked one"; or Antichrist, who shall come. The word used by St Paul in this place signifies "the lawless one,"—the one who is without law, who is not subject to the law of God or of man, whose only law is his own will, to whom the license of his own will is the sole and only rule which he knows or obeys. The Greek word is the lawless, or licentious one. Now, in the book of the prophet Daniel, there is a prophecy, almost identical in terms, where ho foretells that there shall arise in the latter ages of the world a king "who shall do according to his own will" [21] who shall exalt himself above all that is called God, who "shall speak great words against the High one." [22] This is almost word for word the prophecy of St. Paul, which shows us that St. Paul was literally quoting or paraphrasing the prophecy of Daniel. Now, inasmuch as this wicked one shall be a lawless person, who shall introduce disorder, sedition, tumult, and revolution, both in the temporal and spiritual order of the world, so that which shall hinder his development, and shall be his direct antagonist after his manifestation, must necessarily be the principle of order, the law of submission, the authority of truth and of right We therefore have got what I may call an indication to enable us to see where this person, or system which opposes, hinders, or holds the revelation of the man of sin until the sermon shall come, is to be found.

Let us, then, examine the interpretations of the early Fathers on this point Tertullian believed that it was the Roman Empire. The mighty power of pagan Rome, spread throughout the whole world, was the great principle of order which maintained at that time the tranquillity of the earth.

Lactantius who wrote later, maintained exactly the same opinion, and believed that the Roman Empire, which tranquilised and gave order and peace to the nations of the world, thereby hindered the revelation of this lawless one—this man of sin; and both Tertullian and Lactantius enjoined upon the Christians of their time the duty of praying for the preservation of the heathen empire of 'tome, because they believed it to be

---

[21] "Or pleasure" Daniel 11:16
[22] Daniel 7:25

the material barrier against the breaking-in of the great flood of evil which should come upon the world when Rome is destroyed. So also teach St. John Chrysostom and others.

Another interpretation, which is given by Theodoret, a Greek writer, is, that it is the grace of the Holy Ghost, or the Divine power, which retrains the manifestation or the revelation of the man of sin.

Again, other writers say that it is the apostolic power, or the presence of the Apostles; for, as we know from this epistle to the Thessalonians, the Christian were expecting a speedy revelation of the coming of our Lord to judgment, and therefore speedy manifestation of the man of sin; and they believed that the presence of the Apostles upon earth, by their witness and by their miracles, hindered the full manifestation of the principle of unbelief and of spiritual rebellion.

Now these three interpretations am all of them partially true, and all are in perfect harmony one with the other; and we shall find that taken together, they present us with a full and adequate explanation; but these writers, writing at different periods of the Church, were not able fully to understand the prophecy, because the events of the world are continually and progressively interpreting and explaining, from age to age, the meaning of these predict.

1. First. then, the power of the heathen empire of Rome was undoubtedly the great barrier against the outbreak of the spirit of lawless disorder; for, as we know, it was the principle of unity by which the nations of the world were held together. It organised and combined them under the authority of one legislature, of one mighty executive, and of one great sovereignty, with a jurisdiction springing from one fountain, administered by tribunals all ova the world. The peace of nations was maintained by the presence of standing armies; the legions of Rome occupied the circumference of the world. The military roads which sprang from Rome traversed all the earth; the whole world was as it were held peace and in tranquillity by the universal presence of this mighty heathen empire. It was "exceedingly terrible." according to the prophecies of Daniel; it was as it were of iron, beating down and subduing the nations, holding them in subjugation, and thereby, as with a rod of iron, giving prate to the world. There is no doubt that so long as the Roman Empire continued in its strength, it was impossible fir the principle of revolution and disorder to gain head, and therefore these early Christian writers were perfectly cornet in interpreting the hindrance to this spirit of lawlessness to

be the spirit of order, of government, of authority, and of an iron justice which ruled the nations of the world.

2. But, secondly, it was not the Roman Empire, or Rome alone, hut the kingdom of God which descended upon the whole earth, and from the day of Pentecost spread throughout the circuit of the Roman Empire, with an authority higher than the authority of Rome. St Leo gives the basis of this interpretation., He says, "That the effect of this ineffable grace might be diffused throughout the world, he prepared the empire of Rome, the expansion of which was extended to the limits which border upon the whole family of all nations. For it was a fitting preparation for the work divinely disposed that many kingdoms should be confederates in one empire. So that the universal preaching of the Gospel should penetrate speedily through those nations whom the government of one city held in unity!' St. Thomas, resting upon this passage, says that the Roman Empire has not ceased, but is changed from the temporal into the spiritual, commutatum de temporali, in spiritale. Dominicus Soto holds the same opinion. It was, then, the Apostolic Church which, spreading throughout all the nations, already combined together by the power of the heathen empire of Rome, quickened them with a new life, penetrated them with a new principle of order, with a new spirit of unity, consecrated and transfigured the unity of the material forces by which they were held together, gave them one mind, one intelligence, one law, one will, one heart, by the faith which illuminated the intelligence of all nations to know God, by the charity which hound them together in the unity of one family, by the one fountain of jurisdiction which sprang from our divine Lord, and through His Apostles governed the whole earth. There was the one spiritual legislature of the Apostles and their successors. There were tribunals which sat beside the tribunals of Rome. By the side of the tribunals of iron force, were erected the tribunals of divine mercy. This new principle of order, of authority, of submission, and of peace, entered into this world, possessed itself, as I may say, of the material power of the old Roman Empire, and filled it with a new life from heaven. It was the salt of the earth. It prolonged its existence until a certain period, which was foreseen in the predestination of God. It is, therefore, perfectly true that this hindrance signifies also the Holy Ghost; for the Church of God h the presence of the Holy Ghost, incorporated and manifested to the world in the visible body of those who are baptised into the unity of the Church of Jesus Christ.

3. But then, thirdly, it means something still more than this. For these two great powers, spiritual and temporal—the temporal power in the old heathen empire of Rome. and the spiritual power in the new supernatural kingdom of God—met together. They were coincident as it were in their circumference throughout the world; but they met together in their centre, which was in the city of Rome. There they stood, at first face to face, in conflict, then side by side, in peace. There these two mighty powers—the one from earth, and the other from heaven, the one from the will of man, and the other from the will of God—met together as it were in the arena of contest, and for three hundred years the Empire of Rome martyred the pontiffs of the Church of God. For three hundred years the Roman Empire strove to extinguish this new and strange visitant, coming with a superior jurisdiction and with a wider circuit. It strove to destroy it, to quench it in its own blood; and for three hundred years it struggled in vain; for the more the Church was martyred, the more the seed of the martyrs was multiplied. The Church expanded and grew in vigour, in strength, and in power, in proportion as the heathen Empire of Rome strove to extinguish and to destroy it. And this mighty conflict between the two sovereignties at last ended in the conversion of the empire to Christianity, and, therefore, in the enthronement of the Church of God in a supremacy over the powers of the whole world. Then right had power and supremacy over might, and the Divine authority prevailed over the authority of man; then these two powers were blended and fused together: they became one great authority, the emperor ruling from his throne within the sphere of his earthly jurisdiction. and the Supreme Pontiff ruling likewise from a throne of higher sovereignty over the nations of the world, until God in His providence removed the empire from Rome, and planted it upon the shores of the Bosphorus. It departed into the East, and left Rome without a sovereign. Rome from that hour has never had, dwelling within its walls, a temporal sovereign in the presence of the Supreme Pontiff; and that temporal sovereignty devolved by a providential law upon the person of the Vicar of Jesus Christ. It is true, indeed, that in the three centuries between the conversion of Constantine and the period of St. Gregory the Great, in those three centuries of turbulence and disorder, invasion and warfare, by which Italy and Rome was afflicted, the temporal power of the Supreme Pontiff was only in its beginning; but about the seventh century it was firmly established, and that which the Divine Providence had prepared front the beginning received its full manifestation; and no sooner was the material power which once reigned

in Rome consecrated and sanctified by the investiture of the Vicar of Jesus Christ with temporal sovereignty over the city where he dwelt, than he began to create throughout Europe the order of Christian civilisation, Christian empire; Christian monarchies, which, confederated together, have maintained the peace and order of the world from that hour to this. What we call Christendom, that is to say, the great family of Christian nation; Christian races organised and knit together with their princes and their legislatures, by international law, mutual contracts, treaties, diplomacy, and the like, which bind them together in one compact body,— what is this but the security of the world against disorder, turbulence, and lawlessness? And now for these twelve hundred years the peace, the perpetuity, and the fruitfulness of the Christian civilisation of Europe, has been owing solely in its principle to this consecration of the power and the authority of the great Empire of Rome, taken up of old, perpetuated, preserved, as I hare said, by the salt which had been sprinkled from heaven and continued in the person of the Supreme Pontiff, and in that order of Christian civilisation of which he has been the creator.

We hare now come nearly to a solution of that which I stated in the beginning, namely, how it is that the power which hinders the revelation of the lawless one is not only a person but a system, and not only a system but a person. In one word, it is Christendom and its head; and, therefore, in the person of the Vicar of Jesus Christ, and in that twofold authority with which, by Divine Providence he has been invested, we see the direct antagonist to the principle of disorder. The lawless one, who knows no law, human or divine. nor obeys any but his own will, has no antagonist on earth more direct than the Vicar of Jesus Christ, who bears at one and the same time the character of royalty and of priesthood, and represents the two principles of order in the temporal and in the spiritual state—the principle of monarchy, if you will, or of govern- went, and the principle of the apostolic authority. We find, therefore, the three interpretations which I drew out from the Holy Fathers literally verified in this In the slow course of time, as the work of the Apostles matured and ripened, what we call Christendom has arisen, fulfilling the predictions to the letter, manifesting that which the Apostle foretold would hinder the development of this principle of lawlessness, and the revelation of the person who should be its chief.

What, then, is it that at this moment holds in cheek the manifestation of this antichristian power, and the person who shall wield it. It in the remnant of the Christian society which is still existing in the world. There can he but two societies the one natural, the other supernatunal.

The natural society is that political order which comes from the will of man, without relation to the revelation, or the Incarnation of God. The supernatural society is the Church. comprehending those nations which still, being penetrated by the spirit of faith and of the Catholic unity, are true and faithful to the principles upon which Christendom was first constituted.

Ever since the foundation of Christian Europe, the political order of the world has rested upon the Incarnation of our Lord Jesus Christ; for which reason all the public acts of authority, and even the calendar by which we date our dam is calculated from the year of salvation, or from "the year of our Lord." What is the meaning of this phrase, if it be not this, that the state and order under which we lire is based upon the Incarnation; that Christianity is our foundation; that we recognise the revealed laws of God delivered to His incarnate Son, and by the incarnate Son to the Apostles and by the Apostles to the world, us the find principle of nil Christian legislation and of all Christian society. Now this society based upon the Incarnation is the state under which we have hitherto lived. I believe that we are departing from it. We are departing from it throughout the whole of the civilised world. In England, religion is banished from politics. In many countries, such as France, and now in Austria, it is declared by public act that the State has no religion, that all seem are equally participators in the political life and political power of the nation.

I am not now arguing against this. Do not misunderstand me. I state it as a fact. Now a large portion of every nation, and a large portion of France and of Austria, is composed of that race who deny the coming of God in the flesh, that is, who deny the Incarnation. I am not now arguing against their admission to political privileges; on the contrary, I would maintain, that, if there be no other order than the order of nature, it would be a political injustice to exclude any one of the race of Israel from participation of equal privileges; but 1 maintain equally, that in the day in which you admit those who deny the Incarnation to an equality of privileges, you remove the social life and order in which you live from the Incarnation to the basis of mere nature: and this is precisely what was foretold of the antichristian period. We have already seen that the third and special mark of Antichrist is the denial of the Incarnation; and if the nations of the world have been constituted by faith, upon the basis of the Incarnation, the national act which admits those who deny it to a social and political unity, is in the a removal of the order of social life from the supernatural to the natural order: and this is what we see accomplishing. Once more, I say, I am not now arguing against this; but I see in all these facts the verification of prophecy. I am not saying that the political constitution or state of a country should be maintained after the condition of a people renders it morally impossible or difficult. If it is become impossible to maintain this Christian order over a people separated by schism or infected by heresy, or who are mingled with those who deny the Incarnation of God, all that I can say is this, we are reduced to the miserable state of abandoning the true Christian society. This is the dire necessity which falls upon the governments of the world when they depart from the unity and the principles of the Church of Jesus Christ. If such a state cannot be maintained without force, it must be given up. Ecclesia abhorret a sanguine. It is not the spirit of the Church to enforce political problems by sanguinary laws, or to compel unwilling men by the application of physical power. But more is the misery for a people which has so lost faith in the Incarnation. that it is necessary to give up the Christian order instituted by the providence of God. But such is the state of the world, and to this end we are rapidly advancing. We are told that Etna has one hundred and sixty craters. besides the two vast mouths which, joined together, form the immense crater commonly so called, on all its sides it is perforated and honeycombed by channels and by mouths, from which in centuries past the lava has, from time to time, burst forth. I can find no better illustration of the state of Christendom at this moment. The Church of God rests upon the basis of natural society, on the foundations of the old Roman Empire, on the civilisation of the heathen nations of the world, which for a time has been consecrated, consolidated, preserved, raised, sanctified, transformed, by the action of faith and grace. The Church of God rests still upon that basis; but beneath the Church is working continually the mystery of iniquity which already wrought in the Apostles' time, and is culminating at this moment to its strength, and gaining the ascendency. What, I ask, was the French revolution of 1739, with all its bloodshed, blasphemy, impiety, and cruelty, in all its masquerade of horror and of mockery—what was it but an outbreak of the antichristian spirit —the lava front beneath the mountain? And what was the outbreak in 1830 and 1848 but precisely the same principle of Antichrist working beneath Christian society, forcing its way upward? In the year 1848 it opened simultaneously its many mouths in Berlin, in Vienna, in Turin, in Florence, in Naples, and in Rome itself. In London it heaved and struggled; but its time was not yet. What is all this but the spirit of lawlessness lifting itself against God and man,—the principle of schism, heresy. and infidelity running fused into one mass, and pouring itself forth wherever it can force its way, making craters for its stream wherever the Christian society becomes weak? And this, as it has gone on for centuries, so it will go on until the time shall come when "that which holds shall be taken out of the way."

We have already seen what it is that stands in the way of the ascendency of this principle of disorder. Now, visibly, this hindrance or barrier is weakening every day. It is weakening intellectually. The intellectual convictions of men are growing feebler; the Christian and Catholic civilisation is giving way before the natural material which finds its supreme perfection in mere material prosperity; admitting within its sphere persons of every caste, or colour of belief, upon the principle that politics have nothing to do with the world to come, — that the government of nations is simply for their temporal well-being, for the protection of persons and of property, for the development of industry, and for the advancement of science; that is to say, for the cultivation of the natural order alone. This is the theory of civilisation which is becoming predominant every day. Catholic piety also is becoming weaker and weaker, and to such an extent, that there are nations still called Catholic in which the proportion to the mass of those who frequent the Holy Sacraments is hardly calculable: according as our Divine Lord has said, "Because iniquity hath abounded, the charity of many shall grow cold." [23] Again, the Christian society is every where becoming weaker—that is, the true Christian spirit and principle of society. The late M. de Tocqueville, who, as far as I can perceive, had no intention whatever to verify or establish what I am saying, writing upon democracy in America, points out the fact, that the tendency of every government in the world, and of every nation in the world, is to democracy; that is to say, to the diminution and exhaustion of the power of government, and to the development of the license of the popular will, so as to melts all law into the will of the multitude. He points out that in France, in every successive half-century, a double revolution has carried society further towards democracy; that the same phenomena are to be seen in the whole Christian "Every where" he says, "we have seen the events of the life of nations turn to the advancement of democracy; all men have helped it onward by their

---

[23] St Matt. xxiv. 12.

efforts: they who designedly assisted its successes, and they who never thought of serving it; they who have fought for it, and they who are its declared enemies: all have been carried pell-mell in the same path, and all have laboured together; the one sort in spite of themselves, the others without knowing it, as blind instruments in the hand of God.... This whole book has been written under the impression of kind of religious fear produced in the mind of the author by the sight of this irresistible revolution, which for so many centuries marched onward over all obstacles, and which we see still at this day going forward through all the ruins it has made." It is curious to place side by side with this the words of St. Hippolytus, written in the third century, who says that in the end of the world the Roman Empire shall pass into democracies.

Again, another writer, a Spaniard of great intelligence and also of great faith, who lately died ambassador to Paris, Doneso Cortez, describing the state of society, said that Christian society is doomed, that it has to run its course, and become extinct; for the principles which are now in the ascendant are essentially antichristian. He drew out what is most manifest in the history of nations at this moment, namely, that there is a weakening of the principle of the ecclesiastical order every where, and that wheresoever the power of the Church over a nation is weakened, the temporal power is developed in a greater degree; so that nothing is more certain than that temporal despotism prevails especially in those countries where the power of the Church is depressed, and that the only security for liberty among the races of mankind is to be found in the freedom of the Church, and in its free action upon the government of the civil power. He says, "In giving up the empire of faith as dead, and in proclaiming the independence of the reason and of the will of man, society has rendered absolute, universal, and necessary the evil which was only relative, exceptional, and contingent. This period of rapid retrogression commenced in Europe with the restoration of paganism—philosophical, religious, and political. At this day the world is on the eve of the last of its restorations—the restoration of socialist paganism." Again he writes: "European society is dying. The extremities are cold: the heart will be soon. And do you know why it is dying? It is dying because it has been poisoned; because God made it to be nourished with the substance of Catholic truth, and the empirical doctors have given it for food the substance of rationalism. It is dying because, like as man does not live by bread only, but by every word which comes out of the mouth of God, so societies do not perish by the sword only, but by every word which comes out of the mouth of their philosophers. It is dying because error is killing it, and because society is now founded upon errors. Know, then, that all you hold as incontrovertible is false.

"The vital force of truth is so great, that if you were possessed of one truth,—one alone,—that truth might save you. But your fall is so profound, your decline is so radical, your blindness so complete, your nakedness so absolute, that even this one truth you have not. For this reason the catastrophe which must come will be in history the catastrophe above all. Individuals may still save themselves because individuals may always be saved; but society is lost, not because it is yet in a radical impossibility of being saved, but because it has no will to save itself. There is no salvation for society, because we will not make our sons to be Christians, and because we are not true Christians ourselves. There is no salvation for society, because the Catholic spirit, the only spirit of life, does not quicken the whole; it dues not quicken education, government, institutions, laws, and morals. To change the course of things in the state in which they are, I see too well would be the enterprise of giants. There is no power upon earth which, by itself, could reach this end, and hardly all the powers acting together could attain its accomplishment. I leave you to judge whether such cooperation is possible, and to what point, and to decide if, even admitting this possibility, the salvation of society would not be every way a true miracle.

The last point, then, upon which I have to speak is this, that the barrier, or hindrance, to lawlessness will exist until it is taken out of the way. Now what is the meaning of the words, until it "be taken out of the way"? Who is to take it out of the way! Shall it he taken out of the way by the will of man? Shall it be taken out of the way by the mere casualty of events? Surely this is not the meaning. If the barrier which has hindered the development of the principle of antichristian disorder has been the Divine power of Jesus Christ our Lord, incorporated in the Church and guided by his Vicar, then no hand is mighty enough, and no will is sovereign enough to take it out of the way, but only the hand and the will of the incarnate Son of God himself. And, therefore, the interpretation of the Holy Fathers, with which I began, is fully and literally exact. It is the Divine power first in Providence, and then in His Church, and then both fused together, and continuing until the time shall come, the time foreseen and foreordained, for removing the barrier in order to let in a new dispensation of His wisdom upon the earth, upon which I shall have to speak hereafter.

Now we have an analogy to this. The history of the Church, and the history of our Lord on earth, run as it were in parallel. For three-and-thirty years the Son of God incarnate was in the world, and no man could lay hand upon Him. No man could take Him, because His "hour was not yet come." There was an hour foreordained when the Son of God would be delivered into the hand of sinners. He foreknew it; He foretold it. He held it in his own hand, for He surrounded His person with a circle of His own Divine power. No man could break through that circle of omnipotence until the hour came, when by His own will He opened the way for the powers of evil. For this reason He said in the garden, "This is your hour, and the power of darkness." For this reason, before He gave Himself into the hands of sinners, He exerted once more the majesty of His power, and when they came to take Him, He rose and said, "I am He," and "they went backward, and fell to the ground." Having vindicated His divine majesty, He delivered Himself into the hands of sinners. So too, He said, when He stood before Pilate, "Thou shouldst not have any power against Me, unless it were given thee from above" It was the will of God; it was the concession of the Father that Pilate had power over His incarnate Son. Again, He said, "Thinkest thou that I cannot ask My Father, and He will give Me presently more than twelve legions of angels? how then shall the Scripture be fulfilled?" In like manner with His Church. Until the hour is come when the barrier shall, by the Divine will be taken out of the way, no one has power to lay a hand upon it. The gates of hell may war again it; they may strive and wrestle, as they struggle now with the Vicar of our Lord; but no one has the power to more Him one step, until the hour shall come when the Son of God shall permit, for a time, the powers of evil to prevail. That He will permit it for a time stands in the book of prophecy. When the hindrance is taken away, the man of sin will be revealed; then will come the persecution of three years and a half, short, but terrible, during which the Church of God will return into its state of suffering, as in the beginning; and the imperishable Church of God, by its inextinguishable life derived from the pierced side of Jesus, which for three hundred years lived on through blood, will live on still through the fires of the times of Antichrist.

These things are fulfilling fast, and it is good for us to keep them before our eyes: for the forerunners are already abroad—the weakness of the Holy Father, the murder of his armies, the invasion of his States, the betrayal of those who are nearest to him, the tyranny of those who are his sons; the joy, the exultation, the jubilee of Protestant countries and

Protestant governments; the scorn, the contempt, the mockery, which is poured out upon his sacred and anointed head day by day in England And there are Catholics who are scandalised at it; there are Catholics who talk against the temporal power of the Pope, either because they have been stunned by the clamours of a Protestant people, or because they are white-hearted, and have not courage to stand in the face of popular falsehood for an unpopular truth. The spirit of Protestant England—its lawlessness, its pride, its contempt, and its enmity to the Church of God—has made Catholics too to be cold-hearted, even when the Vicar of Jesus Christ is insulted. We have need, then, to be upon our guard. It shall happen once more with some, as it did when the Son of God was in His Passion—they saw Him betrayed, bound, carried away, buffeted, blindfolded, and scourged; they saw Him carrying His Cross to Calvary, then nailed upon it, and lifted up to the scorn of the world; and they said, "If he be the king of Israel, let him now come down from the cross, and we will believe him." So in like manner they say now, "See this Catholic Church, this Church of God, feeble and weak, rejected even by the very nations called Catholic. There is Catholic France, and Catholic Germany, and Catholic Sicily, and Catholic Italy, giving up this exploded figment of the temporal power of the Vicar of Jesus Christ." And so, because the Church seems weak, and the Vicar of the Son of God is renewing the Passion of his Master upon earth, therefore we are scandalised, therefore we turn our facts from him. When then, is our faith? But the Son of God foretold these things when He said, "And now I have told you before it come to pass; that when it shall cons to pass, you may believe."

The Great Apostasy

Before we enter upon the last subject which remains, let us take up the point at which we broke off in the last Lecture. It was this, that there are upon earth two great antagonists—on the one side, the spirit and the principle of evil; and on the other, the incarnate God manifested in His Church, but eminently in His Vicar, who is His representative, the depository of His prerogatives and therefore His special personal witness, speaking and ruling in His name. The office of the Vicar of Jesus Christ contains, in fullness, the Divine prerogatives of the Church: forasmuch as, being the special representative of the Divine Head, he bears all His communicable powers in the government of the Church on earth solely and alone. The other bishops and pastors, who are united with him, and act in subordination to him, cannot act without him; but he may act alone, possessing a plenitude of power in himself. And further, the endowments of the body are the prerogatives of the head and, therefore, the endowments which descend from the Divine Head of the Church upon the whole mystical body are centred in the head of that body upon earth; forasmuch as he stands in the place of the Incarnate Word as the minister and witness of the Kingdom of God among men. Now, it is against that person eminently and emphatically, as said before, that the spirit of evil and of falsehood direct its assault; for if the head of the body be smitten, the body itself must die. "Smite the shepherd, and the sheep shall be scattered," was the old guile of the evil one, who smote the Son of God that he might scatter the flock. But that craft has been once tried, and foiled for ever; for in the death which smote the Shepherd, the flock was redeemed: and through the shepherd who is constituted in the place of the Son be smitten, the flock can be scattered no more. Three hundred years the world strove to cut off the line of the Sovereign Pontiffs; but the flock was never scattered: and so it shall be to the end. It is, nevertheless, against the Church of God, and above all against its Head, that all the spirits of evil in all ages, and, above all, in the present, direct the shafts of their enmity. We see, therefore, what it is that hinders the manifestation, the supremacy, and the dominion of the spirit of evil and of disorder upon earth—namely, the constituted order of Christendom, the supernatural society of which the Catholic Church has been the creator, the bond of union, and the principle of conservation; and the head of that Church, who is eminently the principle of order—the centre of the Christian society which binds the nations of the world in peace. Now the subject which remains to us is far more difficult. It reaches into the future, and deals with agencies so transcendent and mysterious, that all I shall venture to do will be to sketch in outline what the broad and luminous prophecies, especially of the book of Daniel and of the Apocalypse, set forth; without attempting to enter into minute details, which can only be interpreted by the event.

And further, as I said in the beginning, I shall not attempt anything except under the direct guidance of the theology of the Church, and of writers whose works have its approbation. As I have ventured hitherto nothing of my own, so until the end I shall pursue the same course.

What I have, then, to speak of is, the persecution of Antichrist, and finally his destruction.

First of all, let us begin with the twenty-fourth chapter of the holy Gospel according to St. Matthew, in which we read that our Divine Lord said when He beheld the buildings of the Temple, "There shall not be left here a stone upon a stone that shall not be destroyed." And His disciples, when He was in the Mount of Olives, Came to Him privately and said, Tell us what will be the sign of Thy coming, and of the consummation of the world." They understood that the destruction of the Temple in Jerusalem and the end of the world should be part of one and the same action, and should take place at one and the same time. Now, as in nature we see mountains foreshortened one against another, so that the whole chain shares but one form, so in the events of prophecy, there are here two different events which appear but one the destruction of Jerusalem, and the end of the world. Our Divine Lord went on to tell them that there should come such a tribulation as had never yet been; and that unless those days were shortened, there should no flesh be saved; that for the sake of the elect those days should be shortened; that kingdom should rise against kingdom, and nation against nation, and there should be wars and pestilences and famines in divers places; that brethren should betray their brethren to death, (Mark 13) that they should be persecuted for His Name's sake, that all men should hate them, that they should be put to death, and that false Christs and false prophets should arise and should seduce many; that is, there should come false teachers, pretended Messias; and that in the midst of all these persecutions Himself would come to judgment—that, like as the lightning cometh out of the east, and appeareth even unto the west, so shall also the coming of the Son of Man be.

In this answer our Divine Lord spoke of two events—one, the destruction of Jerusalem, and the other, the end of the world. The one has been fulfilled, and the other is yet, to come. This chapter of St. Matthew will afford us a key to the interpretation of the Apocalypse. That book may be divided into four parts. The first part describes the Church on earth, under the seven Churches to which the messages were sent by our Divine Lord. They represent, as a constellation, the whole Church on earth. The second part relates to the destruction of Judaism, and the overthrow of the Jewish people. The third part relates to the persecution of the church by the pagan city of Rome, and to its overthrow: and the fourth and last part relates to the peace of the Church under the figure of the heavenly Jerusalem corning down from heaven and dwelling among men. Many interpreters, especially the early age, and also writers such as Bossuet and others of a later date, have supposed the prophecies of the Apocalypse, excepting only the last chapters, to be fulfilled by the events which took place in the first six centuries—that the overthrow of Jerusalem, the persecution of the Church, and the destruction of pagan Rome. But it is the nature of prophecy gradually to unfold itself. As I said of mountains foreshortened to our sight, when we wind about their base, they begin, as it were, to disentangle their outlines and to reveal themselves as many and distinct; so it is with the events of prophecy. The action of the world moves in cycles; that is, as the wise man says, "what hath been shall be," and "there is nothing new under the sun;" and that which we have seen in the beginning, prophecy declares shall be once more at the end of the world. In the four divisions of the Book Apocalypse, we have seen chief agents: the Church, the Jews, and persecuting power, which was pagan Rome. Now, these three at this moment exist upon earth. There is the Church of God still; there is the ancient people of God, the Jewish race, still preserved, as we have already seen, by a mysterious providence, for some future instrumentality; and there is, thirdly, the natural society of man without God, which took the form of paganism of old, and will take the form of infidelity in the last days. These three arc the ultimate agents in the history of the modern world: first, the natural society of mankind; next, the dispersion of the Jewish people; and, thirdly, the universal Church The two last are the only bodies which interpenetrate into all nations and have an unity distinct and independent of them. They have greater power than any nation, and are deadly and changeless antagonists. Now the Church has had to undergo already two persecutions, one from the hand of the Jews and one also from the hand of the pagans; so the writers of the early ages, the Fathers both of the East and of the West, foretold that, in the last age of the world, the

Church will have to undergo a third persecution, more bitter, more bloody, more searching, and more fiery than any it has undergone as yet, and that from the hands of an infidel world revolted from the Incarnate Word. And therefore the Book Apocalypse, like the prophecy of St. Matthew, reveals two events, or two actions. There is the event which is past, the type and the shadow of the event to come, and there is the event which is still future, at the end of the world; and all the persecutions that have ever been hitherto are no more than the forerunners and the types of the last persecution which shall be.

We have already seen the parallel of the two mysteries, the mystery of impiety and the mystery of godliness; and also the parallel of the two cities, the City of God and the city of this world. There remains another parallel which it is necessary that we should examine in order to make clear that which I shall have to say hereafter. We read in the Book Apocalypse of two women. There is a woman clothed with the sun, and there is a woman sitting upon a beast covered with the names of blasphemy. Now it is clear that these two women, like the two mysteries and the two cities, represent again two antagonist spirits, two antagonist principles. In the twelfth chapter of the Book Apocalypse we read of the woman "clothed with the sun," having "the moon under her feet, and on her head a crown of twelve stars." No Catholic will be at a loss for an interpretation of these words; and even Protestant interpreters, in order to avoid seeing the immaculate Mother of God in this woman clothed with the sun, tell us that it signifies the Church. In this they are perfectly right, —only they speak but half the truth. The woman typifies or symbolises the Church, for this reason, that the symbol of the Church is the Incarnation, the woman with the child; the symbol of the Incarnation is the Mother of God. On the other hand, we need not go far to find the interpretation of the woman who sits upon the beast having the names of blasphemy, for the last verse of the seventeenth chapter says "The woman which thou sawest is the great city which hath kingdom over the kings of the earth." It is quite clear, then, the there is an antagonism between these two women — the Church under the symbol of the Incarnation, and the great city, the city of Rome, with the seven hills, which has kingdom over the kings the earth.

Now let us keep clearly in mind this distinction because interpreters, heated by the spirit of controversy, have been pleased to confound these two things together, and to tell us that this woman seated on the beast is the Church of Rome. But the Church of Rome is the Church of God, or least a part of it, even in the mind of these interpreters. How, then, can these two, which so contrary the one to the other, mean the same thing? In truth, as it was with Elymas magician, who, for his perverseness, could not hold the sun for a season, so they who heat themselves in controversy lose their sense. In the splendor of this vision they cannot see the truth, and about to find the Church of God in that which the type of its antagonist; fulfilling again the end self-deceit, that when the truth is upon earth mistake a falsehood for the truth, as when the true Christ was come, they knew Him not, and called Him Antichrist. As it was with His Person, so it is with His Church.

With these preliminary distinctions, let us begin the last part of our subject. What I have to speak of is the persecution which Antichrist shall inflict upon the Church of God. We have already seen reason to believe that as our Divine Lord delivered Himself into the hands of sinners when His time was come, and no man could lay hand upon Him, until of His own free will He delivered Himself over to their power, so in like manner it shall be with that Church of which He said, "Upon this rock will I build my Church, and the gates of hell shall not prevail against it." As the wicked did not prevail against Him even when they bound Him with cords, dragged Him to the judgment, blindfolded His eyes, mocked Him as a false King, smote Him on the head as a false Prophet, led Him away, crucified Him, and in the mastery of their power seemed to have absolute dominion over Him, so that He lay ground down and almost annihilated under their feet; and as, at that very time when He was dead and buried out of their sight, He was conqueror over all, and rose again the third day, and ascended into heaven, and was crowned, glorified, and invested with His royalty, and reigns supreme, King of kings and Lord of lords,—even shall it be with His Church: though for a time persecuted, and, to the eyes of man, overthrown and trampled on, dethroned, despoiled, mocked, and crushed, yet in that high time of triumph the gate of hell shall not prevail. There is in store for the Church of God a resurrection and an ascension, a royalty and a dominion, a recompense of glory for all it has endured. Like Jesus, it needs must suffer on the way to its crown; yet crowned it shall be with Him eternally. Let no one, then, be scandalised if the prophecy speak of sufferings to come. We are fond of imagining triumphs and glories for the Church on earth,—that the Gospel is to be preached to all nations, and the world to be converted, and all enemies subdued, and I know not what, —until some ears are impatient of hearing that there is in store for the Church a time of terrible trial: and so we do as the Jews of old, who looked for a conqueror, a king, and for prosperity; and when their Messias came in humility and in passion, they did not know Him. So, I am afraid, many among us intoxicate their minds with the visions of success and victory, and cannot endure the thought that there is a time of persecution yet to come for the Church of God. Let us hear, therefore, the words of the prophet Daniel. Speaking of the person whom St. John calls the Antichrist, whom he calls the king that shall work according to his own will, the prophet Daniel says, "He shall speak words against the High One,"—that is, the Almighty God,—"and shall crush the saints of the Most High." Again he says, "It"—that is, the power of this king—"was magnified even unto the strength of heaven: and it threw down of the strength, and of the stars and trod upon them. And it was magnified even to the prince of the strength: and it took away from him the continual sacrifice, and cast down the place of his sanctuary." Further, he says, "The victim and the sacrifice shall fail, and there shall be in the temple the abomination of desolation." These three passages are taken from the seventh, and the eighth, and the ninth chapters of Daniel. I might add more, but they are enough, for in the Book Apocalypse (12:7) we find a key to these words. St. John, evidently referring to the Book of Daniel, writes of the beast, that is, the persecuting power which shall reign on the earth by might, "It was given unto him to make war with the saints and to overcome them." Now here we have four distinct prophecies of a persecution which shall be inflicted by this antichristian power upon the Church of God. I will therefore point out as briefly as I can what appears in the events now around us to be leading on to this result.

1. The first sign or mark of this coming persecution is an indifference to truth. Just as there is dead calm before a whirlwind, and as the waters over a great fall run like glass, so before an outbreak there is a time of tranquillity. The first sign is indifference. The sign that portends more surely than any other the outbreak of a future persecution is a sort of scornful indifference to truth or falsehood. Ancient Rome in its might and power adopted every false religion from all its conquered nations, and gave to each of them a temple within its walls. It was sovereignly and contemptuously indifferent to all the superstitions of the earth. It encouraged them; for each nation had its own proper superstition, and that proper superstition was a mode of tranquillising, of governing, and of maintaining in subjection, the people who were indulged by building a temple within its gates. In like manner we see the nations of the Christian world at this moment gradually adopting every form of religious contradiction—that is, giving it full scope, and, as it is called, perfect

toleration; not recognising any distinctions of truth or falsehood between one religion or another, but leaving all forms of religion to work their own way. I am not saying a word against this system if it be inevitable. It is the only system whereby freedom of conscience is now maintained. I only say, miserable is the state of the world in which ten thousand poisons grow round one truth; miserable is the state of any country where truth is only tolerated. This is a state of great spiritual and intellectual danger; and yet it seems there is no alternative but that the civil governors leave perfect freedom of conscience, and therefore maintain themselves in a state of perfect indifference.

Let us see the result. First of all, the divine voice of the Church of God is thereby entirely ignored. They see no distinction between a doctrine of faith and a human opinion. Both are allowed to have free way. There are mixed together doctrines of faith with every form of heresy, until, as in England, we have all conceivable forms of belief, from the Council of Trent in all its rigour and in all its perfection, on the one hand, to the *Catechism of Positive Religion* on the other. We have every form of opinion started, and freely allowed, from the two extremes; the one of which is the worship of God in Unity and Trinity, incarnate for us; and the other, the denial of God, and the worship of humanity. Next, denying and ignoring of course the divine voice of the Church, the civil governor must ignore the divine unity of the Church, and admit every form of separation, or system, or division all mingled together; so that the people are crumbled into religious sects and religious divisions, and the law of unity is entirely lost. Then, again, all positive truth, as such, is despised; and it is despised, because who shall say who is right and who is wrong, if there be no Divine teacher? If there be no Divine judge, who shall say what is true and what is false between conflicting religious opinions? A state that has separated itself from the unity of the Church, and thereby has lost the guidance of the Divine teacher, is unable to determine by any of its tribunals, civil or ecclesiastical. as it may continue to call them, what is true and what is false in a controverted question of religion; and then, as we know, there grows up an intense hatred of what is called dogmatism, that is, of any positive truth, any thing definite, any thing final, anything which has precise limits, any form of belief which is expressed in particular definitions—all this is utterly distasteful to men who on principle encourage all forms of religious opinion. In fact, we are coming to the state of Festus, who, when he heard that the Jews had an accusation against St. Paul, reported that he could find "no question which seemed ill" to him, because they were questions superstition, and "about one Jesus deceased, whom Paul affirmed to be alive." [24] Now this is just the state of indifference to which the civil governors of the world are gradually reducing themselves, and the government they administer, and the people they govern.

2. The next step is, then, the persecution of the truth. When Rome in ancient days legalised every idolatry throughout the whole of the Roman Empire, there was one religion which was called a religio illicita, an unlawful religion, and there was one society which was called a societas illicita, or an unlawful society. They might worship the twelve gods of Egypt, or Jupiter Capitolinus, or Dea Roma; but they might not worship the God of heaven, they might not worship God, revealed in His Son. They did not believe in the Incarnation; and that one religion which was alone true was the only religion that was not tolerated. There were the priests of Jupiter, of Cybele, of Fortune, and of Vesta; there were all manner of sacred confraternities, and orders, and societies, and I know not what; but there was one society which was not permitted to exist, and that was the Church of the living God. In the midst of this universal toleration, there was one exception made with the most peremptory exactness, to exclude the truth and the Church of God from the world. Now this is what must again inevitably come to pass, because the Church of God is inflexible in the mission committed to it. The Catholic Church will never compromise a doctrine; it will never allow two doctrines to be taught within its pale; it will never obey the civil governor pronouncing judgment in matters that are spiritual. The Catholic Church is bound by the Divine law to suffer martyrdom rather than compromise a doctrine, or obey the law of the civil governor which violates the conscience; and more than this, it is not only bound to offer a passive disobedience, which may be done in a corner, and therefore not detected, and because not detected not punished; but the Catholic Church cannot be silent; it cannot hold its peace; it cannot cease to preach the doctrines of Revelation, not only of the Trinity and of the Incarnation, but likewise of the Seven Sacraments, and of the infallibility of the Church of God, and of the necessity of unity, and of the sovereignty, both spiritual and temporal, of the Holy See; and because it will not be silent, and cannot compromise, and will not obey in matters that are of its own Divine prerogative, therefore it stands alone in the world; for there is not another Church so called, nor any community

---

[24] Acts 20:18-19

professing to be a Church, which does not submit, or obey, or hold its peace, when the civil governors of the world command. It is not ten years since we heard of a decision on the matter of baptism, involving the doctrine of original sin on the one hand, and the doctrine of preventing grace on the other; and because a civil judge pronounced that it was lawful in the Established Church of England for men without punishment to teach two contradictory doctrines, bishops, priests, and people were content that it should be so: or, at least, they said, "We cannot do otherwise; the civil power will allow men to preach both: what can we do? We are persecuted, and therefore we hold our peace; we go on ministering under a civil law which compels us to endure that the man who preaches before us in the morning, or the man who shall preach after us in the afternoon, may preach a doctrine in diametrical contradiction to that which we know to be the revealed doctrine of God; and because the civil governors have determined it so, we are not responsible, and the Established Church is not responsible, because it is persecuted." Now this is the characteristic difference between a human system established by the civil law and the Church of God. Would it be permitted in the Church which is Catholic and Roman, that I should now deny that every child baptised receives the infusion of regenerating grace? What would become of me by tomorrow morning? You know perfectly well that if I were to depart one jot or one tittle from the Holy Catholic faith, delivered by the Divine voice of the Church of God, I should be immediately suspended. and no civil governor, or power in the world, could restore me to the exercise of my faculties; no civil judge or potentate on earth could restore me to the administration of the Sacraments, until the spiritual authority of the Church permitted me to do so.

This, then, is the characteristic difference, which must one day bring down upon the Church, in all countries where this spirit of indifference has established itself, a persecution of the civil power. And for a further reason, because the difference between the Catholic Church and every other society is this other societies are of voluntary formation; that is, people unite themselves to a particular body, and, they do not like it on better knowledge, they go their way: they become Baptists, or Anabaptists, or Episcopalians, or Unitarians, or Presbyterians, until they find something which they do not like in these stems; and then they go their way, and either unite themselves to some other body or remain unattached; because the societies have no claim to govern the will,—all that they profess to do is to teach. They are like the ancient school, and their teaching is a kind of Christian philosophy. They put their doctrines before those who are willing to listen, and if they listen, and, by good fortune agree with them, they remain with them: if not. they go their way. But where is the government over the will? Can they say, "In the name of God, and under pain of mortal sin, you must believe that God was incarnate, and that our incarnate Lord offers Himself in sacrifice upon the altar, that the Sacraments instituted by the Son of God are seven, and that they all convey the grace of the Holy Ghost" Unless they have an authority over the will as well as over the intelligence, they are only a school, and not a kingdom. Now this is a character entirely wanting in every society that cannot claim to govern in the name of our Divine Lord, and with a Divine voice and therefore the Church of God differs from every other society in this particular, that it is not only a communion of people who voluntarily unite together, but that it is a kingdom, It has a legislature; the line of its councils for eighteen hundred years have deliberated, and decreed with all the solemnity and the majesty of an imperial parliament. It has executive which carries out and enforces the decree of those councils with all the calmness and all the peremptory decision of an imperial will. The Church of God, therefore, is an empire within an empire; and the governors and princes of this world are jealous of it for that very reason. They say, "Nolumus hunc regnare super nos"—"we will not have this man to reign over us" It is precisely because the Son of God, when He came, established a kingdom upon earth, that therefore, in every land, in even nation, the Catholic Church governs with the authority of the universal Church of God. For instance, in England, the little and despised flock of Catholics united together under a hierarchy of ten years old, resting upon the Holy See as its centre, speaks and governs with a sovereignty derived from the whole Church of God. Therefore it is that ten years back the atmosphere was rent and tormented by the uproar of "Papal aggression." The natural instinct of the civil rulers knew that it was not a mere Christian philosophy wafted from foreign lands, but a government, a power, and a sovereignty. For this reason also, the extreme liberal school —those who claim toleration for every form of opinion, and who teach that the office of the civil governor is never to enter into controversies of religion, but that all men should be left free in their belief, and the conscience of all men be at liberty before God—even they make one exception, and, in the strangest contradiction to all their principles, or, at least, their professions. maintain that as the Catholic Church is not only a form of doctrine, but also a power or government, it must be excepted from the general toleration. And this is precisely the point of future collision. It is the very reason why the Archbishops of Cologne, Turin, Cagliari, and the like, went the other day into exile; why nineteen Sees are, at this moment, vacant in Sardinia. Why, in Italy, Bishops are, at this day, cast out from their Episcopal thrones: it is for this reason that in this land the Protestant religion is established instead of Catholic truth, and that thrones once filled by the Bishops of the universal Church are now occupied by those whom the royalties of England, and not the royalties of the Vicar of Jesus Christ, have chosen and set up. It is the same old contest, old as Christianity itself, which has been from the beginning, first with pagan, and then with heretic, and then with schismatic, and then with infidel, and will continue to the end. The day is not far off, when the nations of the world, now so calm and peaceful in the stillness of their universal indifference, may easily be roused, and penal laws once more may be found in their Statute-books.

3. This leads on plainly to the marks which the prophet gives of the persecution of the last days. Now there are three things which he has recorded. In the foresight of prophecy he saw and noted these three signs. The first, that the continual sacrifice shall be taken away; the next, that the sanctuary shall be occupied by the abomination which maketh desolate; the third, that "the strength" and "the stars," as he described it: shall be cast down: and these are the only three I will notice.

Now, first of all what is this "taking away of the continual sacrifice"?

It was taken away in type at the destruction of Jerusalem. The sacrifice of the Temple, that is, of the lamb, morning and evening, in the Temple of God, was entirely abolished with the destruction of the Temple itself. Now the Prophet Malachias says: "From the rising of the sun even to the going down, any name is great among the Gentiles; and in every place there is sacrifice, and there is offered to my name a clean oblation." This passage of the prophet has been interpreted by the Fathers of the Church. beginning with St. Irenaeus, St. Justin Martyr, and I know not how many besides, to be the sacrifice of the Holy Eucharist, the true Paschal lamb which came in the place of the type—namely, the sacrifice of Jesus Himself on Calvary renewed perpetually and continued for ever in the sacrifice on the altar. Now has that continual sacrifice been taken away? That which was typical of it in old days has been already taken away. But has the reality been taken away? The holy Fathers who have written upon the subject of Antichrist, and of these prophecies of Daniel, without a single exception, as far as I know, and they are the Fathers both of the East and of the West, the Greek and the Latin Church—all of them unanimously,—say that in the latter end of the world, during the reign of Antichrist, the holy sacrifice of the altar will cease. In the work on the end of the world, ascribed to St. Hippolytus, after a long description of the afflictions of the last days, we read as follows: "The Churches shall lament with a great lamentation, for there shall be offered no more oblation, nor incense, nor worship acceptable to God. The sacred buildings of the churches shall be as hovels; and the precious body and blood of Christ shall not be manifest in those days; the Liturgy shall be extinct; the chanting of psalms shall cease; the reading of Holy Scripture shall be heard no more. But there shall be upon men darkness, and mourning upon mourning, and woe upon woe. Then, the Church shall be scattered, driven into the wilderness, and shall be for a time, as it was in the beginning, invisible, hidden in catacombs, in dens, in mountains, in lurking-places; for a time it shall be swept, as it were, from the face of the earth. Such is the universal testimony of the Fathers of the early centuries. Has there ever come to pass anything which may be called an installment or a forerunner of such an event as this? Look into the East. Mahometan superstition, which arose in Arabia, swept over Palestine and Asia Minor, the Seven Churches, and Egypt, the north of Africa—the home of St. Augustine, St. Cyprian, St. Optatus—and finally penetrated into Constantinople, soon it became dominant, has in every place persecuted and suppressed the worship and sacrifices of Jesus Christ. The Mahometan superstition at moment holds for its mosques a multitude of Christian churches, in which the continual sacrifice is already taken away, and the altar utterly destroyed. In Alexandria and in Constantinople there stand churches built for Christian worship, into which the foot of no Christian has ever entered since the continual sacrifice has been swept away. Surely in this we see, in part at least, the fulfilment of this prophecy; so much so, that many interpreters will have it that Mahomet is the Antichrist, and that none other is to come. No doubt he was one of the many forerunners and types of the Antichrist that shall be. Now let us look into the Western world: has the continual sacrifice been taken away in any other land? — for instance, in all those churches of Protestant Germany which were once Catholic, where the holy sacrifice of the Mass was daily offered! — throughout Norway, and Sweden, and Denmark, and one half of Switzerland, where there are a multitude of ancient Catholic churches — through England, in the cathedrals and the parish churches of this land, which were built simply as shrines of Jesus incarnate in the Holy Eucharist, as sanctuaries raised for the offering of the Holy Sacrifice? What is the characteristic mark of the Reformation, but the rejection of the Mass, and all that belongs to it, as declared in the Thirty-nine Articles of the Church of England to be blasphemous fables and dangerous deceits? The suppression of the continual sacrifice is, above all, the mark and characteristic of the Protestant Reformation. We find, then, that this prophecy of Daniel has already its fulfilment both the East and West,—in the two wings, as it were while in the heart of Christendom the Holy Sacrifice is offered still. What is the great flood of infidelity, revolution, and anarchy, which is now sapping the foundations of Christian society, not only in France, but in Italy, and encompassing Rome, the centre and sanctuary of the Catholic Church, but the abomination which desolates the sanctuary, and takes away the continual sacrifice? The secret societies have long ago undermined and honeycombed the Christian society of Europe, and are at this moment struggling onward toward, Rome, the centre of all Christian order in the world. The fulfilment of the prophecy is yet to come; and that which we have seen in the two wings, we shall see also in the centre; and that great army of the Church of God will, for a time, be scattered. It will seem, for a while, to be defeated, and the power of the enemies of the faith for a time to prevail. The continual sacrifice will be taken away, and the sanctuary will be cast down. What can be more literally the abomination which makes desolate than the heresy which has removed the presence of the living God from the altar? [25] If you would understand this prophecy of desolation, enter into a church: which was once Catholic, where now is no sign of life; it stands empty, untenanted, without altar, without tabernacle, without the presence of Jesus. And that which has already come to pass in the East and in the West is extending itself throughout the centre of the Catholic unity.

    The Protestant spirit of England, and the schismatical spirit even of countries Catholic in name. is at this moment urging on the great

---

[25] Saint Alphonsus says: "Hence St. Bonaventure says that in the Mass God manifest to us all the love that He has borne us, and includes in it, as in a compendium, all His benefits. On this account the Devil has always endeavored to abolish the Mass throughout the world by means of heretics, making them the precursors of Antichrist who, before all things, will endeavor to abolish, and in fact will, in punishment for the sins of men, succeed in abolishing the Holy Sacrifice of the Altar, according to the prediction of Daniel: 'And strength was given him against the continual sacrifice because of sins.'"

anticatholic movement of Italy. Hostility to the Holy See is the true and governing motive. And thus we come to the third mark, the casting down of "the Prince of Strength;" that is, the Divine authority of the Church, and especially of him in whose person it is embodied, the Vicar of Jesus Christ. God has invested him with sovereignty, and given to him a home and a patrimony on earth. The world is in arms to depose him, and to leave him no place to lay his head. Rome and the Roman States are the inheritance of the Incarnation. The world is resolved to drive the Incarnation off the earth. It will not suffer it to possess so much as to set the sole of its foot upon. This is the true interpretation of the anticatholic movement of Italy and England: "Tolle hunc de terra." The dethronement of the Vicar of Christ is the dethronement of the hierarchy of the universal Church, and the public rejection of the Presence and Reign of Jesus.

4. Nor, if I am obliged to enter somewhat into the future, I shall confine myself to tracing out very general outline. The direct tendency of all the events we see at this moment is clearly this, to overthrow Catholic worship throughout the world. Already we see that every Government in Europe is excluding religion from its public acts. The civil powers are desecrating themselves: government is without religion; and if government be without religion, education must be without religion. We see it already in Germany and in France. It has been again and again attempted in England. The result of this can be nothing but the re-establishment of mere natural society; that is to say, the governments and the powers of the world, which for a time were subdued by the Church of God to a belief in Christianity, to obedience to the laws of God, and to the unity of the Church, having revolted from it and desecrated themselves, hare relapsed into their natural state

The Prophet Daniel, in the twelfth chapter, says that in the time of the end "many shall be chosen and made white, and shall be tried as fire; and the wicked shall deal wickedly, and none of the wicked shall understand, but the learned shall understand;" that is, many who have known the faith shall abandon it, by apostasy. "Some of the learned shall fall;" (Daniel 11:33) that is, they shall fall from their fidelity to God. And how shall this come to pass? Firstly by fear, partly by deception, partly by cowardice, partly because they cannot stand for unpopular truth in the face of popular falsehood; partly because the overruling contemptuous public opinion, as in such country as this, and in France, so subdues and frightens Catholics, that they dare not avow their principles, and, at last, dare not hold them. They become admirers and worshipers of the material prosperity of Protestant countries. They see the commerce, the manufacture, the agriculture, the capital, the practical science, the irresistible armies, and the fleets that cover the sea, and they come flocking to adore, and say, "Nothing is so great as this great country of Protestant England." And so they give up their faith, and become materialists, seeking for the wealth and power of this world, dazzled and overpowered by the greatness of a country which has cast off its fidelity to the Church.

5. Now the last result of all this will be a persecution, which I will not attempt to describe. It is enough to remind you of the words of our Divine Master: "Brother shall betray brother to death:" it shall be a persecution in which no man shall spare his neighbour, in which the powers of the world will wreak upon the Church of God such a revenge as the world before has never known. The Word of God tells us that towards the end of time the power of this world will became so irresistible and so triumphant that the Church of God will sink underneath its hand — that the Church of God will receive no more help from emperors, or kings, or princes, or legislatures, or nations, or peoples, to make resistance against the power and the might of its antagonist. It will be deprived of protection. It will be weakened, baffled, and prostrate, and will lie bleeding at the feet of the powers of this world. Does this seem incredible? What, then, do we see at this moment? Look at the Catholic and Roman Church throughout the world. When was it ever more like its Divine Head in the hour when He was bound hand and foot by those who betrayed Him? Look at the Catholic Church, still independent, faithful to its Divine trust, and yet cast off by the nations of the world; at the Holy Father, the Vicar of our Divine Lord, at this moment mocked, scorned, despised, betrayed, abandoned, robbed of his own, and even those that would defend him murdered. When, I ask, was the Church of God ever in a weaker condition, in a feebler state in the eyes of men, and in this natural order, than it is now? And from whence, I ask, is deliverance to come? Is there on earth any power to intervene? Is there any king, prince, or potentate, that has the power to interpose either his will or his sword for the protection of the Church? Not one; and it is foretold it should be so. Neither need we desire it, for the will of God seems to be otherwise. But there is One Power which will destroy all antagonists; there is One Person who will break down and smite small as the dust of the summer threshing-floor all the enemies of the Church, for it is He who will consume His enemies "with the Spirit of His mouth," and destroy them "with the brightness of His

coming." It seems as if the Son of God were jealous lest any one should vindicate His authority. He has claimed the battle to Himself; He has taken up the gage which has been cast down against Him; and prophecy is plain and explicit that the last overthrow of evil will be His; that it will be wrought by no man, but by the Son of God; that all the nations of the world may know that He, and He alone, is King, and that He, and He alone, is God. We read in the Book Apocalypse of the city of Rome, that she said in the pride of her heart, "I sit as a queen, and am no widow, and sorrow I shall not see. Therefore shall her plagues come in one day, death, and mourning, and famine, and she shall be burned with the fire, because God is strong who shall judge her." Some of the greatest writers of the Church tell us that in all probability, in the last overthrow of the enemies of God, the city of Rome itself will he destroyed; it will be a second time punished by Almighty God, as it was in the beginning. There was never destruction upon earth comparable to the overthrow of Rome in ancient days. St. Gregory the Great, writing of it, says, "Rome a little while ago was seen to be the mistress of the world; what she now is we behold. Crushed by manifold and boundless miseries, by the desolation of her inhabitants, the inroads of enemies, the frequency of destruction, we set fulfilled in her the words of the Prophet against the city. Where is the senate; where now is the people? The bones are decayed, and the flesh is consumed. All the pomp of worldly greatness in her is extinguished. Her whole structure is dissolved. And we, the few who remain, are day by day harassed by the sword and by innumerable tribulations. Rome is empty and burning; ... her people have failed, and even her walls are falling ... Where now are they who once exulted in her glory? Where is their pomp; where their pride; where their constant and immoderate rejoicing?" There never was a ruin like to the overthrow of the great City of the Seven Hills, when the words of the prophecy were fulfilled: "Babylon is fallen"—like "a great millstone cast into the sea"

The writers of the Church tell us that in the latter days the city of Rome will probably become apostate from the Church and Vicar of Jesus Christ; and that Rome will again be punished, for he will depart from it; and the judgment of God will fall on the place from which he once reigned over the nations of the world. For what is it that makes Rome sacred, but the presence of the Vicar of Jesus Christ? What has it that should be dear in the sight of God, save only the presence of the Vicar of His Son? Let the Church of Christ depart from Rome, and Rome will be no more in the eye of God than Jerusalem of old. Jerusalem, the Holy City, chosen by

God, was cast down and consumed by fire, because it crucified the Lord of Glory; and the city of Rome, which has been the seat of the Vicar of Jesus Christ for eighteen hundred years, if it become apostate, like Jerusalem of old, will suffer a like condemnation. And, therefore, the writers of the Church tell us that the city of Rome has no prerogative except only that the Vicar of Christ is there; and if it become unfaithful, the same judgments which fell on Jerusalem, hallowed though it was by the presence of the Son of God, of the Master, and not the disciple only, shall fall likewise upon Rome.

The apostasy of the city of Rome from the Vicar of Christ, and its destruction by Antichrist, may be thoughts so new to many Catholics, that I think it well to recite the text of theologians in the greatest repute. First, Malvenda, who writes expressly on the subject, states as the opinion of Ribera, Gaspar Melus, Viegas, Suarez, Bellarmine and Bosius, that Rome shall apostatise from the faith and drive away the Vicar of Christ, and return to its ancient paganism. Malvenda's words are: "Rome itself in the last times of the world will return to its ancient idolatry, power, and imperial greatness. It will cast out its Pontiff, altogether apostatise from the Christian faith, terribly persecute the Church, shed the blood of martyrs more cruelly than ever, and will recover its former state of abundant wealth, or even greater than it had under its first rulers."

Lessius says: "In the time of Antichrist, Rome shall be destroyed, as we see openly from the thirteenth chapter of the Apocalypse;" and again: "The woman whom thou sawest is the great city, which hath kingdom over the kings of the earth, in which is signified Rome in its impiety, such as it "as in time of St. John, and shall be again at the end of the world." And Bellarmine "In the time of Antichrist, Rome shall be desolated and burnt, as ye learn from the sixteenth verse of the seventeenth chapter of the Apocalypse." On which words the Jesuit Erbermann comments as follows: "We all confess with Bellarmine that the Roman people, a little before the end of the world, will return to Paganism, and drive out the Roman Pontiff."

Viegas, on the eighteenth chapter of the Apocalypse, says: "Rome, in the last age of the world, after it has apostatised from the faith, will attain to great power and splendour of wealth, and its sway will he widely spread throughout the world, and flourish greatly. Living in luxury and the abundance of all things, it will worship idols, and be steeped in all kinds of superstition, and will pay honeur to false gods. And because of the vast effusion of the blood of martyrs which war shed under the emperors, God will most severely and justly avenge them, and it shall be utterly destroyed, and burned by a most terrible and afflicting conflagration."

Finally, Cornelius A. Lapide sums up what may be said to be the common interpretation of theologians. Commenting on the same eighteenth chapter of the Apocalypse, he says: "These things are to be understood of the city of Rome, not that which is, nor that which was, but that which shall ho at the end of the world. For then the city of Rome will return to its former glory, and likewise its idolatry and other sins, and shall be such as it was in the time of St. John, under Nero, Domitian, Decius, etc. For from Christian it shall again become heathen. It shall cast out the Christian Pontiff, and the faithful who adhere to him. It shall persecute and slay them. It shall rival the persecutions of the heathen emperors against the Christians. . . . . For so we see Jerusalem was first heathen under the Canaanite; secondly, faithful under the Jews; thirdly, Christian under the Apostles; fourthly, heathen again under the Romans; fifthly, Saracen under the Turks."

Such they believe will be the history of Rome: pagan under the emperors, Christian under the Apostles, faithful under the Pontiffs, apostate under the Revolution, and pagan under Antichrist. Only Jerusalem could sin so formally and fall so low; for only Jerusalem has been so chosen, illumined, and consecrated. And as no people were ever so intense, in their persecutions of Jesus as the Jews, so I fear will none ever be more relentless against the fair than the Romans.

Now I have not attempted to point out what shall be the future events except in outline, and I have never ventured to designate who shall be the person who shall accomplish them. Of this I know nothing; but I am enabled with the most perfect certainty, from the Word of God, and from the interpretations of the Church, to point out the great principles which are in conflict on either side I began by showing you that the Antichrist, and the antichristian movement, has these marks: first, schism from the Church of God; secondly, denial of its Divine and infallible voice; and thirdly, denial of the Incarnation. It is, therefore, the direct and mortal enemy of the One Holy Catholic and Roman Church—the unity from which all schism is made; the sole organ of the Divine voice of the Spirit of God; the shrine and sanctuary of the Incarnation and of the continual sacrifice.

And now to make an end. Men have need to look to their principles. They have to make a choice between two things, between faith in a teacher speaking with an infallible voice, governing the unity which now, as in the beginning, knits together the nations of the world, or the spirit of fragmentary Christianity, which is the source of disorder and ends in unbelief. Here is the simple choice which we are all brought; and between them we must make up our minds.

The events of every day are carrying men further and further in the career on which they have entered. Every day men are becoming more and more divided. These are times of sifting. Our Divine Lord is standing in the Church: "His fan is in His hand, and He will thoroughly cleanse His and He will gather the grain into His barn, and will burn up the chaff with unquenchable fire." It is a time of trial, when "some of the learned shall fall," and those only shall be saved who is steadfast to the end. The two great antagonists are gathering their forces for the last conflict;—it may not be in our day, it may not be in the time of those who come after us; but one thing is certain, that we are as much put on our trial now as they will he who live in the time when it shall come to pass. For as surely as the Son of God reigns on high, and will reign "until He has put all His enemies under His feet," so surely every one that lifts a heel or directs a weapon against His faith, His Church, or His Vicar car upon earth, will share the judgment which is laid up for the Antichrist whom he serves.

THE END.

From Saint Pius X Press

The Religious State by Saint Alphonsus Ligouri $11.95

Vocations by Fr. William Doyle S.J. $9.95

Readings For Each Sunday In The Year: The Catholic Mother To Her Children by the Countess de Flavigny $9.95

History of the Church, Formation of the Apostles of the Latter Times by Phil Friedl $9.95

Night Adoration in the Home $6.95 Note we are preparing a simpler presentation a lower cost. This will be available for bulk ordering. Please contact us for details.

Guide to General Confession with Examination of Conscience $9.95

Saint Pius X Press
Box 74
Delia KS 66418
www.stpiusxpress.com

Our thanks to www.divineprovidenceweb.com for cover design and formatting this book.

Made in the USA
Middletown, DE
04 August 2016